Excommunicating the Faithful:
Jewish Christianity in the Early Church

Excommunicating the Faithful:
Jewish Christianity in the Early Church

Kenneth W. Howard

An Imprint of the
Global Center for Religious Research
1312 17TH Street • Suite 549
Denver, Colorado 80202

INFO@GCRR.ORG • GCRR.ORG

GCRR Press
An imprint of the Global Center for Religious Research
1312 17th Street Suite 549
Denver, CO 80202
www.gcrr.org

DOI: 10.33929/GCRRPress.2022.01

Typesetter: Hannah Purtymun, Jennifer Walker
Copyeditor: Erika Spong
Proofreader: Kelcey Morgan Norris
Cover Image: Madaba Mosaic Map of Jerusalem, Sixth Century CE
Cover Design: Abdullah Al Mahmud
                    fiverr.com/mahmuddidar

Library of Congress Cataloging-in-Publication Data

Excommunicating the faithful: Jewish Christianity in the early church /
Kenneth W. Howard
p.   cm.
Includes bibliographic references (p.)
ISBN (Print): 979-8-9857300-8-1
ISBN (eBook): 979-8-9857300-9-8
1. Church history—Primitive and early church, ca. 30–600.   2. Jewish
Christianity—Primitive and early church, ca. 30–600.   3. Heresies,
Christian—History—Early church, ca. 30–600.   4. Judaism—History—
Post-exilic period, 586 B.C.–210 A.D.   I. Title.

BS2840.E4   .H693   2022

CB

For my great-grandfather, Rabbi Reuben Minkoff of Mogilev in Belarus, who died long before I was born yet is my exemplar of faithful ministry.

Advanced Endorsements

Here is a thorough study that elucidates a grievous turn in church history while analyzing the roots of Christian antisemitism. It also offers a cautionary tale for all Christian polity. Tracing the brave polity of inclusion of the apostolic age to its demise three centuries later, *Excommunicating the Faithful* is especially relevant in today's febrile mix of religion, politics, and culture. It's message reminds us that, given the right set of circumstances, the oppressor and the oppressed can easily switch places, even among the followers of Jesus of Nazareth.

–The Reverend Peter M. Antoci, PhD
Dean, Southern Maryland Region,
Episcopal Diocese of Washington

What happened to Jewish Christianity in the first centuries of the Christian church? Largely due to a dearth of original material, this proves to be a very difficult question to answer. Focusing on the fate of several of the more "orthodox" early Jewish Christian sects, Ken Howard's *Excommunicating the Faithful* is an impressive attempt to extract an answer to this question from the fragmentary and often problematic source material available.

–Morgan Rempel, PhD
Department of Philosophy and Religious Studies,
Georgia Southern University

Contents

Abbreviations

ad Gal.	Ambrosiaster, *commentarius in epistulam ad Galatas* ("Commentary on the Epistle to the Galatians")
adv. haer.	Irenaeus. *adversus haereses* ("Against Heresies"), aka *The Panerion* ("The Bread Basket")
adv. Luc.	Jerome. *adv. Lucianus* ("Against Lucian")
adv. Marc.	Tertullian. *adversus Marcionem* ("Against Marcion")
adv. omn. haer.	Pseudo-Tertullian. *adversus omnes haereses* ("Against All Heresies")
adv. Paleg.	Jerome. *adversus Palegius* (Against Palegius)
anacor.	Epiphanius. *Anacortus* ("The Anacortes")
Antioch	Athanasius. *canonum superius memorata Synodus Antiochiae in Syria* ("Canons of the Synod at Antioch in Syria")
apol.	Justin Martyr. *próti sygnómi* ("First Apology")
archeology	Mancini, Ignazio. *Archeological Discoveries Relative to the Jewish-Christians.* Jerusalem: Franciscan, 1970.
Av. Zar.	*Avodah Zara* ("Foreign Worship"), Talmud (Babylonian)
B. Brach	Babylonian Talmud, Berakhot ("Blessing")

B. Gittin	Babylonian Talmud, *Gittin* ("Documents")
c. Celsum	Origen. *contra Celsum.* ("Against Celsus')
c. Cres.	Augustine. *contra Cresconium grammaticum partis Donati* ("Against Cresconius, a Donatist Grammarian")
chron.	Eusebius. *chronicon* ("Chronicle")
chron. Pasch.	Author unknown. *chronicon Paschale* (the "Paschal Chronicle" or "Easter Chronicle"), also called *chronicum Alexandrinum, Constantinopolitanum,* or *fasti siculi*
Const.	Eusebius. *vita Constantini* ("The Life of Constantine")
de bapt.	Augustine. *de baptismo contra Donatistas* ("On Baptism, Against the Donatists")
de carne.	Tertullian. *de carne Christi* ("The Body of Christ")
de praesc.	Tertullian. *de praescriptione haereticorum* ("The Prescription Against Heretics")
de princ.	Origen. *de principiis* ("On First Principles")
de situ	Jerome. *de situ et nominibus locorum hebraicorum liber* ("On locations and local names in the Hebrew Scriptures")
de vir. Ill.	Jerome. *de viris illustribus* ("On Illustrious Men")
de virg. vel.	Tertullian. *de virginibus velandis* ("On the Veiling of Virgins")
dem.	Araphrat of Persia. *Demonstrations* (translated from the original Syriac)
Dial.	Justin Martyr. *Dialogue with Trypho the Jew*
div. haer. liber.	Philastrius (also Philaster or Filaster). *diversarum hereseon liber* ("Book of Diverse Heresies")

epist.	Jerome. epistola Augustini ("Epistle 79 to Augustine")
hist. eccl.	Eusebius. *Historia Ecclesiastica* ("Church History")
hom. in Gen.	Origen. *homiliae in Genesim* ("Homilies on Genesis"). Latin translation by Jerome.
hom. in Jer.	Origen. *homiliae in Jeremias* ("Homilies on Jeremiah"). Latin translation by Jerome.
hom. in Luc.	Origen. *homiliae in Lucam* ("Homilies on Luke"). Latin translation by Jerome.
in epist. ad Rom.	Origen. *in epistulam ad Romanos* ("On the Epistle to the Romans")
in epist. ad Titum	Chrysostom. *in epistulam ad Titum* ("On the Epistle to Titus")
in Esaiam	Eusebius. *commentarium in Esaiam* ("Commentary on Isaiah")
in Hab.	Jerome. *commentarium in Habakkuk* ("Commentary on Habakkuk")
in Hiez.	Origen. *homiliae in Hiezechielem* ("Commentary on Ezekiel")
in Joh.	Origen. *commentarium in evangelium Ioannis* ("Commentary on the Gospel of John")
in Matth.	Origen. *commentarium in evangelium Matthaei* ("Commentary on the Gospel of Matthew")
in Mic.	Jerome. *commentarium in Micah* ("Commentary on Micah")
Jud.	Chrysostum. *adversus Judaeos* ("Against the Jews")

Nazarene	Pritz, Raymond A. *Nazarene Jewish-Christianity: From the End of the New Testament Period until Its Disappearance in the Fourth Century.* Jerusalem: Magnes, 1988.
onomas.	Eusebius. *onomasticon* (*peri tōn topikōn onomatōn tōn en tē Theia Graphē*), ("On the Place-Names in the Holy Scripture")
pan	Epiphanius. *panerion* ("The Bread Basket"), aka *Adversus Haereses* ("Against Heresies")
Pascha	Melito, *peri Pascha* ("Homily on the Passion")
PE	A. F. J. Klijn and G. J. Reinink, *Patristic Evidence of Jewish Christian Sects.* (Leidon, Netherlands: Brill).
PEAJ	Wilson, Stephen G. "Passover, Easter, and Anti-Judaism: Melito of Sardis and Others." In Jacob Neusner and Ernest S. Frerichs (eds.), *"To See Ourselves as Others See Us": Christians, Jews, "Others" in Late Antiquity*, 337–355. Chico, CA: Scholars Press, 1955.
phil.	Ignatius. *epistolí stous philadélfeia* ("Epistle to the Philadelphians")
Praef.	Origen. *praefatio contra Celsum.* ("Preface of Against Celsus")
prol.	Jerome. *commentarium de nominibus Hebraicis* (prologus), ("Prologue to the Commentary on Hebrew Names")
ref.	Hippolytus. *refutatio omnium haeresium* ("Refutation of All Heresies"), aka *Elenchus* or *Philosophumena*
refut. omn. haer.	Hippolytus. *refutatio omnium haeresium* ("Refutation of All Heresies"), aka *Elenchus* or *Philosophumena*
Sanh.	Babylonian Talmud, *Sanhedrin* ("The Synod")

Sota	Babylonian Talmud, *Sota* ("Errant Wife")
Strom.	Clement. *Stromata* ("Miscellanies")
Taanit	Babylonian Talmud, *Taanit* ("Fasting")
Theo.	Theodotion. *Septuagint* ("Seventy"). Greek translation of the Hebrew Scriptures.
War.	Josephus. *o evraïkós pólemos* ("The Jewish War")
Weights	Epiphanius. *métra kai stathmá* ("Weights and Measures")

Introduction and Thesis

I. Introduction

The study of Jewish Christianity in the early church is both intriguing and disheartening. It goes without saying that all of the first Christians were Jews. Jesus's disciples, the Twelve, and the Apostle Paul were all Jews. The book of Acts reports that tens of thousands "from the circumcision" came to believe in Jesus as Messiah.[1] None are recorded as ever renouncing their Judaism. In fact, the controversial issue at the time was quite the opposite. The earliest church council was called by the Apostles to determine whether a person could become a follower of Jesus without first converting to Judaism. Yet by the early part of the second century, if the reports of the church fathers are to be believed, all that remained of Jewish Christianity were small, isolated pockets of Jewish Christians.[2] Some were relatively orthodox in their theology.

---

[1] Acts 21:20; cf. Joseph A. Fitzmyer, "Jewish-Christianity in Acts in the Light of the Qumran Scrolls," in *Essays on the Semitic Background of the New Testament*, (London: Geoffrey Chapman, 1971): 271–304. Fitzmyer notes that great care must be exercised in the use of the book of Acts in order to distinguish "Lucan theologoumena" from the historical information that it also contains. While the Acts account is problematic in establishing specific events as historic, it tends to be more helpful in establishing the context within which Jewish Christianity arose. Readers may give more weight to the historical assertions of Acts when they have points of contact from other sources, biblical or non-biblical. For example, Fitzmyer has established a number of points of contact between the book of Acts and the Qumran materials.

[2] Ernest W. Saunders, "Jewish Christianity and Palestinian Archeology," *Religious Studies Review* 9 (3) (1983): 201–205; cf. Bellarmino Bagatti, *The Church from the Circumcision: History and Archaeology of the Judaeo-Christians* (Jerusalem: Franciscan Printing Press, 1971); Ignazio Mancini, *Archaeological Discoveries Relative to the Judaeo-Christians,*

Some occupied the fringe of orthodox Christian doctrine. Some were beyond the fringe. However, orthodox or not, they were held in almost universally low esteem by the larger church, judging by the opinions of most of the patristic writers—which demonstrate an ambivalence at best. By the end of the fourth or fifth centuries, Jewish Christianity had apparently disappeared; if the patristic literature is to be believed, there are no contemporaneous reports on any Jewish Christian sects after that time.

This work will trace the development of Jewish Christianity from its beginnings in the earliest Christian communities through its eventual apparent disappearance. It will attempt to shed light on several questions: Who were the various groups which composed, or which evolved from Jewish Christianity? What can be said of their origins and development, and what became of them? What were the natures of the theologies—particularly the Christologies— of these various groups? How did the attitude of the church fathers toward Jewish Christianity change from the first to the fourth century? And how did their changing attitudes contribute toward the eventual demise of Jewish Christianity?

These questions are difficult to answer with certainty because original source materials are extremely scarce. No original Jewish Christian documents currently exist in complete form. All that remain are fragments of Jewish Christian documents—a few Gospels and scriptural commentaries—quoted by various patristic writers. The only other sources of information on early Jewish Christianity are the reports of the patristic writers themselves, the majority of which are either secondhand or based on tradition. There are also several canonical and apocryphal documents which are thought to be dependent on earlier Jewish Christian documents or which display aspects of Jewish Christian theology. Therefore, this

---

(Jerusalem: Franciscan Printing Press, 1970); and G. Quispel, "The Discussion of Judaic Christianity," *Vigiliae Christianae* 22 (1968): 81. Bagatti and Mancini believe that the archaeological evidence indicates that Jewish Christianity was much more prevalent in the third and fourth centuries than is apparent from patristic sources, and was perhaps the dominant form until the arrival of the Byzantines. Quispel argues that Jewish Christianity remained alive and active long after the fall of Jerusalem and was instrumental in spreading Christianity to Mesopotamia and further east, laying the groundwork for Aramaic-speaking, Syrian Christianity.

paper will draw on a variety of sources including biblical evidence, fragments of Jewish Christian documents as quoted in patristic documents, the comments of the patristic writers themselves, and certain early Jewish documents.

II. Thesis

The author's thesis is that within the diversity which characterized the Jewish Christianity of the early church, there existed at least one Jewish Christian sect whose theology stood within the acceptable bounds of orthodoxy of the church, and that this sect existed through at least the fourth century—at which point it was declared heretical by the church fathers and eventually died out, despite the fact that it remained within the bounds of orthodoxy[3] and considered itself a part of the greater church. The thesis also suggests that the increasing antipathy of the church fathers toward Jewish Christianity was the result of a variety of interrelated influences operating over several centuries. Some of these influences included: the changing demographics of the church and the accompanying clash of cultures; the increasing isolation of Jewish Christianity from the predominantly Gentile church; power struggles between competing Christian communities in Palestine, as well as Rome's interest in asserting its primacy; theological and pastoral concerns— which were well-intentioned but resulted in increasingly narrow views of orthodoxy and orthopraxy; as well as some outright anti-Jewish attitudes.

Care must be taken in applying the term "orthodoxy" in this context to avoid its application in an anachronistic manner. For example, it would be inappropriate to apply modern standards of orthodoxy to the period of the early church covered by this investigation. Furthermore, within the period covered by this investigation it would be equally inappropriate to apply the standards of orthodoxy of a later period to an earlier period (e.g., the more unified orthodoxy of the fourth-century post-Nicaea church to the diversity of the first-century primitive church). Therefore, when

---

[3] That is, orthodox in all ways except for its observance of the ceremonial law.

the term orthodox is applied to a group in this study, it is applied in context; that is, in terms of the acceptable standards of orthodoxy present in the greater church at the time (e.g., second-century Jewish Christian groups will be evaluated against the standards of orthodoxy of the second-century church).

III. Defining Jewish Christianity: A Review of the Literature

A major problem in the study of Jewish Christianity is defining the subject. Some scholars tend to define Jewish Christianity very broadly, in primarily theological terms. For example, Danielou speaks of Jewish Christianity as Christianity expressed in the thought-forms of Judaism; in other words, Christian groups whose theology was dependent on the theological concepts and symbols of Judaism.[4] Similarly, Longenecker, following Danielou, defines Jewish Christians as those Christian communities which existed between 20 CE and 135 CE and which were located in Jerusalem or considered Jerusalem to be their mother church.[5] Quispel, using a similarly broad definition, classifies the beginnings of Christianity in Syria, Alexandria, and North Africa as Jewish Christian.[6] While such a broad concept of Jewish Christianity has the benefit of demonstrating the deep roots of Christianity in the theological concepts of Judaism at the time, it is too broad to permit any meaningful study and inevitably leads to statements such as those by Klijn—that early Christianity was a Jewish Christian phenomenon.[7] While such a statement is undoubtedly true, it does not limit the field of study in any useful way.

---

[4] Jean Danielou, *The Development of Christian Doctrine before the Council of Nicaea*, Vol.1, The Theology of Jewish-Christianity (Chicago: Regnery, 1964), 10.

[5] R. N. Longenecker, *The Christology of Early Jewish Christianity* (London: SCM Press, 1970); quoted in G. Lüdemann, *Opposition to Paul in Jewish Christianity* (Philadelphia: Fortress, 1989), 29.

[6] Quispel, 81.

[7] A. F. J. Klijn, "The Study of Jewish-Christianity," *New Testament* 20 (1973/74): 426.

Some scholars continue to use the term "Jewish Christian" in an ethnic sense, although not as frequently as in years past. Defined ethnically, a Jewish Christian is a member of the Christian community born of Jewish parents. Adolf von Harnack, for instance, took such an approach.[8] A solely ethnic perspective, while certainly narrowing the field of study, is overly simplistic. For example, it would be inappropriate for the purposes of this study to classify as Jewish Christian a person who had renounced all connections to all aspects of Jewish ceremony and theology.

Schoeps and others define Jewish Christianity in terms of orthodoxy and heresy.[9] This involves taking at face value the categories imposed by the early Christian heresiologists. By this definition, the Jewish Christians of the earliest Jerusalem church are accepted as orthodox, while groups which appear on later lists of heresies are a priori considered heretical. Lüdemann notes that while this approach has enjoyed great popularity since the time of Eusebius, it is relatively uncritical and seldom attempts to define the concept of Jewish Christianity in any practical way.[10]

Finally, Simon, Lüdemann, and others argue that Jewish Christianity should be defined primarily in a religious sense. In this case, Jewish Christians are considered to be those members of the Christian church with a commitment to the ceremonial law, regardless of their ethnic origins.[11] This approach views Jewish Christianity primarily as an anti-Pauline movement.[12] It includes Gentile Christians who were committed to the ceremonial law and excludes per se those of Jewish background who were not. While this position avoids the overly broad generalizations of Danielou's

---

[8] Adolf von Harnack, *History of Dogma Vol. 1*, translated by Neil Buchanan (1958). Quoted in Lüdemann, 30.

[9] Hans-Joachim Schoeps, *Jewish-Christianity: Factional Disputes in the Early Church* (Philadelphia: Fortress, 1964), 9–13.

[10] Lüdemann, 30.

[11] Marcel Simon, *Versus Israel: A Study of the Relations between Christians and Jews in the Roman Empire*, trans. H. McKeating (New York: Oxford University Press, 1986), 265f, 390ff; cf. Lüdemann, 30.

[12] Simon, *Versus Israel,* 247f. However, Simon does not claim that Jewish Christianity was univocal in its anti-Paulinism. Rather, the tenor of each Jewish Christian group's anti-Paulinism was dependent on the group's attitude toward the law.

definition without the gross oversimplification of a strictly ethnic approach or the narrowness of the orthodoxy/heresy approach, it too has some disadvantages.

For one thing, Lüdemann argues that the Apostle Paul should not be considered a Jewish Christian because he did not observe the Torah in his associations with Gentiles. Yet Paul never spoke of himself as a convert from Judaism[13]—he believed faith in Christ to be the true successor of the faith of Abraham.[14] He may have been willing to observe the ceremonial law in his dealings with Jews,[15] and he was willing to require Jewish ethics of Gentile converts.[16] Therefore, it would be inappropriate to define Jewish Christianity in a way that would exclude him. In addition, it is not true that Jewish Christianity was a uniformly anti-Pauline phenomenon since (as I

---

[13] Gal 1:15ff; cf. Phil 3:4ff. In Paul's own account of his coming to faith in Christ he never calls himself a proselyte nor does he use the term conversion to describe his experience. Rather, he speaks of his experience as a calling. Even in his letter to the Philippians, in which he accounts all his achievements as a devout Jew as loss and irrelevant to his salvation, he does not renounce his Jewishness or speak of himself as an ex-Jew.

[14] Rom 4:1ff; cf. Patrick J. Hartin, "Jewish Christianity: Focus on Antioch in the First Century," *Scriptura* 36 (1991): 50.

[15] Cor 9:19ff; cf. Acts 21:23–26; 1 Cor 11:19ff; Gal 2; Albrecht Ritschl, *The Formation of the Old Catholic Church* (1857), quoted in Lüdemann, 12–13. The Acts passage, in which Paul agrees to observe the purification rituals while in Jerusalem, is historically problematic for the reasons mentioned above. However, in 1 Cor 9:19ff Paul proclaims his willingness to be as a Gentile to Gentiles and as a Jew to Jews. While this can be interpreted in other ways, it does allow the possibility that Paul was willing to observe the law occasionally, as a means to an end: winning Jews to Christ. Also, in 1 Cor 11:19ff Paul seems to have adopted the Jewish Passover ritual as the model for the Lord's Supper. On the basis of Gal 2 it can be argued that for Paul occasionally to submit to ceremonial law, after criticizing Peter for his inconsistency in the application of the ceremonial law, would amount to violating his own principle. However, Ritschl argues that Paul understood the apostolic decree geographically; that is, churches outside of Palestine would fall under Paul's authority, while those inside would fall under the authority of James and Peter. If this was the case, then Paul would have been living up to the terms of his agreement and acknowledging the authority of James and Peter when he submitted to the purification rituals.

[16] George P. Carras, "Jewish Ethics and Gentile Converts: Remarks on 1 Thess 4:3–8," in *The Thessalonian Correspondence*, ed. Raymond F. Collins (Leuven, Belgium: Leuven University Press, 1990): 306–315.

will argue below) at least one Jewish Christian group, the Nazarenes, did accept Paul and his Gentile mission. Finally, this perspective does not adequately represent the variety of attitudes towards the ceremonial law by those who did observe it: those who practiced it on certain occasions but not on others; those who observed it to honor the Jewishness of the Lord Jesus;[17] and those who viewed it as essential for salvation.

The effort to formulate a comprehensive but specific definition of Jewish Christianity seeks a uniformity of theology and practice which did not exist at the time. Modern scholarship has established that first-century Judaism was not a monolithic movement but had a variety of competing strands of theology and practice. It is naïve to assume that the followers of Christ who emerged from these Jewish strands would not demonstrate a similar diversity. Perhaps a more pragmatic approach to the definition of Jewish Christianity would be most appropriate. Such an approach would broadly recognize as Jewish Christian any group of people who considered themselves to be Jewish and who also considered themselves to be followers of Christ. It would then organize these groups according to appropriate subcategories: by their attitude toward ceremonial law, Christology, etc. Such a modified ethnic definition would eliminate from study those Gentile Christian groups who appropriated Jewish theological concepts or even ceremonial concepts without specifically identifying themselves as Jewish. It would also eliminate from consideration those ethnic Jews who renounced all identification with Judaism. For example, groups like the Nazarenes, who practiced the ceremonial law consistently (not as a legal requirement for salvation, but to honor the Jewishness of Jesus Christ), would be considered law-observant, orthodox Jewish Christians. Those like the Apostle Paul, who considered themselves free from the requirements of the ceremonial law, but did not renounce their identification with Judaism, would be considered law-free, orthodox Jewish Christians. However, groups like the Ebionites, whose theology (I will argue below) fell outside

---

[17] Origen, *in Matth.* Ser. 79, in A.F.J. Klijn and G.J. Reinink, *Patristic Evidence for Jewish Christian Sects.* (Leiden, Netherlands: Brill), 13, referred to in subsequent notes as *PE*.

the bounds of orthodoxy, would be considered law-observant, heretical Jewish Christians. And the Elkesaites, who (I will argue below) adopted some Jewish Christian ideas but did not acknowledge Jesus as the Messiah and did not consider themselves a part of the greater church, would be considered a Jewish group, albeit a syncretistic one, and not Jewish Christian.

IV. Survey of Sources

The definition of the term Jewish Christian has no small impact on the issue of sources. The modified ethnic definition of Jewish Christianity adopted by this study allows more focused attention to be given to a more manageable number of closely related groups and sources than would be possible with Danielou's diffusive definition. In addition, sources for this study are limited, for the most part, to sources which can shed light on specific, identified Jewish Christian groups. However, some attention is given to documents which cannot be attributed to a specific group, but which nonetheless establish important background information on Jewish Christianity.

A. Biblical Sources

The term Jewish Christian is not used in the New Testament. However, the book of Acts does provide some light on the context and origins of Jewish Christianity. The Bible will be one of the major sources of background data for "Chapter I—Background: Analysis of the Biblical, Archaeological, and Other Data."

B. Jewish Christian Gospels
and Related Documents

Jewish Christian groups left behind little direct literary evidence. What remains are fragments of documents which are quoted by the patristic authors. Jewish Christian groups produced several non-canonical Gospels. Although these have all been referred to by the patristic authors as the *Gospel According to the Hebrews*, these are actually at least two or three different recensions of the *Gospel According to Matthew*, each associated by patristic authors with a different Jewish Christian group.[18] Not only is this evidence fragmentary, but there is also some confusion over which document fragments should be associated with which group. Therefore, great care must be taken in using this evidence. The Jewish Christian gospel materials will be the primary focus of "Chapter III—The Theology of the Jewish Christians: Analysis of the Jewish Christian Gospels."

In addition to these Gospel fragments, fragments from the Nazarene *Commentary on Isaiah*[19] are useful in documenting certain aspects of that group's theology. The *Pseudo Clementine* literatures, specifically the *Homilies* and *Recognitions*, are helpful in establishing the theological concepts of the Ebionites. Information from these sources will be included in "Chapter II—Who Were the Jewish Christians? Examination of the Candidates Suggested by the Church Fathers" and "Chapter IV—Corroborating the Church Fathers: Analysis of Archaeological, Talmudic, and Other Sources."

Other writings, which cannot be attached to a specific Jewish Christian group, but which may be used to establish characteristics of early Jewish Christianity, include the *Didache*, the *Epistle of Barnabas*, the *Shepherd of Hermas*, and others. Information from these sources will be found in "Chapter I—Background: Analysis of Biblical References and Early Church Documents."

C. Apologetic and Patristic Literature

Most of the information available on early Jewish Christianity comes from the Apologetic and patristic literature. For many reasons, great care must be taken in evaluating this information. It is in no way comprehensive. It is not the direct product of Jewish Christian groups. Many of these reports are not eyewitness reports but secondhand information. Not least important is the fact that these are the reports of the "winning side," those who in the end declared all Jewish Christian groups to be heretical, and therefore may be subject to some self-justification. Nevertheless, they form

---

[18] P. Vielhauer and G. Strecker, "Jewish-Christian Gospels" in *New Testament Apocrypha. Vol. 1, Gospels and Related Writings.* ed. W. Schneemelcher (Philadelphia: Fortress, 1991) 134–178.

[19] Jerome, *in Esaiam* (*PE*, 109).

the largest part of what limited information is available, and so they must be used.

Information from Apologetic and patristic sources will be found primarily in "Chapter III—The Theology of the Jewish Christians: Analysis of the Jewish Christian Gospels." Some of the major writers quoted include Justin Martyr, Irenaeus, Tertullian, Hippolytus, Pseudo-Tertullian, Eusebius, Epiphanius, Jerome, and Augustine. Secondary studies which were important in the development of this section include Klijn's and Reinink's *Patristic Evidence for Jewish Christian Sects*, Pritz's *Nazarene Jewish Christianity*, Vielhauer and Strecker's "Jewish-Christian Gospels," and Lüdemann's *Opposition to Paul in Jewish Christianity*.[20]

D. Jewish Talmudic Literature

A study of Jewish Christianity would not be complete without consulting early Jewish sources for potential information, though many researchers have neglected to do so. Part of the problem lies with the difficulty in using Talmudic texts, in any precise manner, for historical evidence. In the case of Jewish Christianity, the references are few: about a dozen Talmudic texts. Primary sources for this data include Pritz's *Nazarene Jewish Christianity* and Schiffman's *Who Was a Jew?*[21] However, the Talmudic texts do provide some useful corroborative evidence, which is offered in "Chapter IV—Corroborating the Church Fathers: Analysis of Archaeological, Talmudic, and Other Sources."

---

[20] Klijn and Reinink, *PE*; Raymond A. Pritz, *Nazarene Jewish Christianity: From the End of the New Testament Period until Its Disappearance in the Fourth Century* (Jerusalem, Israel: Magnes Press, 1988); Vielhauer and Strecker; cf. Lüdemann.

[21] Lawrence H. Schiffman, *Who Was a Jew? Rabbinic and Halakhic Perspectives on the Jewish Christian Schism.* (Hoboken. NJ: Ktav Publishing House, 1985).

E. Archaeological and Historical Sources

Archeological sources provide some useful information about the prevalence and geographic extent of Jewish Christianity in Palestine and the surrounding areas in the first four centuries—the period covered by this study. A primary source for this data will be Mancini's work *Archaeological Discoveries Relative to the Judaeo-Christians*,[22] with some supplementary data from other sources. This data will be covered in "Chapter II—Background: Analysis of Biblical References and Early Church Documents" and "Chapter IV: Corroborating the Church Fathers." Chapter V will also draw on historical data from Josephus's *Jewish Wars*. Boyarin's book, *Borderlines: The Partition of Judeo-Christianity*,[23] Fredrickson's book, *When Christians Were Jews: The First Generation*,[24] and Reed's book, *Jewish-Christianity and the History of Judaism*[25] also provide useful historical context for Chapter IV, as well as "Chapter V—From Acceptance Through Ambivalence to Antipathy: The Changing Attitude of the Church Fathers toward Jewish Christianity."

---

[22] Mancini, *Archaeology*.

[23] Daniel Boyarin, *Borderlines: The Partition of Judeo-Christianity* (Philadelphia: University of Pennsylvania Press, 2006).

[24] Paula Fredriksen, *When Christians Were Jews: The First Generation* (New Haven, CT: Yale University Press, 2018).

[25] Annette Yoshiko Reed, *Jewish-Christianity and the History of Judaism* (Heidelberg, Germany: Mohr Siebeck, 2017).

1

Background:
Analysis of Biblical References
and Early Church Documents

The Bible, while it provides no information on any specific Jewish Christian groups, does provide useful background information about the context out of which Jewish Christianity and the primitive Christian church emerged. Similarly, analysis of early church documents can provide additional useful contextual information.

I. Biblical References

The Scriptures themselves do not shed much light on the specific subject of Jewish Christianity, but they do provide valuable background information. The book of Acts records that in the earliest days of the church, all believers were Jews; that is, they observed the requirements of the Jewish ceremonial law.[23] In fact, until the council at Jerusalem there appeared to be an assumption that Gentiles wishing to become followers of Jesus would have to agree first to follow the requirements of the Jewish ceremonial law—in effect, converting to Judaism. The council determined that Gentiles could become followers of Jesus without first becoming Jews.[24] Later, a wide variety of local church communities evolved:

---

[23] Acts 2:5ff. One would assume that they did not treat the ceremonial law as essential to salvation.

[24] Acts 15:1–35; cf. Gal 2:7ff; Albrecht Ritschl, *The Formation of the Old Catholic Church* (1857), quoted in Lüdemann, 12–13. As previously noted, Ritschl argues that Paul understood the Apostolic decree geographically; that is, churches outside of Palestine would fall under Paul's authority (and would be free from the requirement to observe the ceremonial law), while those inside would fall under the authority of James and Peter.

some mixed Jew/Gentile, some almost entirely Gentile, and some composed almost entirely of Jews. Of the Jewish believers, many appear to have been law-observant.[25]

The New Testament records several names given to the early church: The Way,[26] Nazarenes,[27] and Christians.[28] In the book of Acts story, the prosecutor Tertullus accuses Paul of being "a ringleader of the sect of the Nazarenes."[29] While it is possible that Tertullus could have invented the Nazarenes for the occasion, this seems unlikely for three reasons. First, Paul does not deny that such a sect exists.[30] Second, the name "Nazarene" (Heb. *Nozri/Nozrim*) is used in some Talmudic literature, in which the incidents described may have happened, as early as 110 CE.[31] Third, several patristic writers confirm that both the terms "Nazarenes" and "Christians" were early names applied to the followers of Christ and that they were in use at the same time.[32] Even if the incident described in the Acts story was non-historical, the story itself makes it clear that the term "Nazarene" would have been accepted by the earliest Christians as an appropriate name for themselves.

If this is true, then it seems quite possible that these three terms may have represented two branches of the church as early as 57 CE (the approximate date of Paul's trial).[33] The term "Nazarene"

---

[25] Acts 15:1; 21:20; Gal 2:4; 5:12.

[26] Acts 9:2; 18:25,26; 19:9,23; 24:14,22; cf. Joseph A. Fitzmyer, "Jewish-Christianity in Acts in the Light of the Qumran Scrolls," in *Essays on the Semitic Background of the New Testament* (London: Geoffrey Chapman, 1971): 271–304. Fitzmyer notes that the Qumran community also employed the term "The Way" as a name for itself, so the term may have been familiar to the early Christian community.

[27] Acts 24:5.

[28] Acts 11:26; cf. Acts 26:28; 1 Pet 4:16.

[29] Acts 24:5; cf. Epiphanius, *pan.* 29.6.2 (*PE*, 171).

[30] Acts 24:5ff; cf. Epiphanius, *pan.* 29.6.3–5 (*PE*, 171).

[31] *b av. Zar.* 16b–17a, Pritz, *Nazarene*, 96. Pritz dates the *terminus ad quem* of this text at no later than 130 CE, given the appearance of R. Eliezer b. Hyrkanos, but suggests that the fact that it mentions the arrest of R. Eliezer, which occurs about 109 CE, means the text may have originated even earlier.

[32] Tertullian, *adv. Marc.* 4.8 (*PE*, 109); cf. Eusebius, *onomas.* (*PE*, 151); Epiphanius, *pan.* 29.1.3; 6.2ff (*PE*, 169); Jerome; *de situ* 143 (*PE*, 207).

[33] Cf. Pritz, *Nazarene*, 11ff.

may have been used at first by opponents of the early church as a derogatory term for the church as a whole (viewed then as a sect of Judaism). Meanwhile, church members (all Jewish Christians at that time) may have referred to themselves as "disciples of the Way." Similarly, "Christian," a Greek name, was first used at Antioch, which was probably the first Gentile mission. It was first used by non-believing Gentiles as a contemptuous term for followers of Christ. It seems plausible that as the term "Christian" came to be exclusively identified with Gentile believers, "Nazarene" would have continued to be applied in Palestine as a term for Jewish believers in Christ.[34]

It should be noted here that the book of Acts reveals Luke's tendency to present a picture of the early church that minimizes the conflict between Paul and the other Apostles which led to the Jerusalem Council. Acts tends to portray Paul in a Petrine manner and Peter in a Pauline manner. Baur argues on this basis that Acts was the product of a Paulinist in Rome who wished to minimize the differences between Peter and Paul, to defend Paul against the objections of Jewish Christians, and to make possible a rapprochement between the Paulinist and Jewish Christian factions in Rome. He speculates that by the second and third generations, the various Christian factions in Rome found themselves faced with the need to draw closer together, and that Acts was an attempt to provide a basis for such a consensus.[35]

The Gospel According to Matthew provides another view into Jewish Christianity in the early church. There are a number of reports from the church fathers that the various Jewish Christian groups used one of several different gospels which were called by the name "Gospel According to the Hebrews," each of which was related in some degree to the canonical Gospel According to Matthew.[36] The Nazarene Jewish Christians had a gospel, written in Aramaic or Hebrew, which (as I will demonstrate later) was very

---

[34] Pritz, *Nazarene*, 14–15.

[35] Ferdinand Baur, *Paul, the Apostle of Jesus Christ: His Life and Work, His Epistles and His Doctrine*, 1845, trans. A. Menzies (Peabody, MA: Hendrickson Publishers, 2003), quoted in Lüdemann, 5–6.

[36] Vielhauer and Strecker, 134ff. Various authors distinguish either two or three different gospels called by this name by the church fathers.

close to the canonical Matthew—so close, in fact, that many researchers believe it originated in the same line of tradition which produced the canonical version.[37] On the other hand, the Ebionite Jewish Christians had a different gospel, written in Greek, which was related to the canonical Matthew in some respects, but differed greatly in others, containing some heretical material.[38]

Most modern commentators agree that the author of the canonical Matthew was a second-generation Jewish Christian writing around 90 CE in or near Antioch in Syria. This was a time following the rabbinic reorientation of Judaism at Yavne, after which Jewish Christians had either left or were excluded from the synagogues. The author was, in one sense, attempting to provide his predominantly Jewish Christian community with an alternative to rabbinical authority by portraying Jesus as the new Moses and the church as the new Israel.[39] Matthew's church appears to be taking a middle ground: positioning itself as both a part of the greater church, by opening itself to the Gentile mission,[40] while at the same time positioning the church as the legitimate heir to and fulfillment of God's promises to Israel by emphasizing the ethical aspects of Christianity.[41] Clearly, Matthew's congregation expressed a tension which was common to early Jewish Christianity: on the one hand, they considered themselves followers of Christ; on the other hand, they believed that they remained Jews.[42]

---

[37] Vielhauer and Strecker, 157ff. Some, pointing to certain Aramaic/Hebraic expressions, take the Nazarene version to be an earlier, more primitive version of Matthew. Most, pointing to potential textual emendations (e.g., doublings, etc.) take it to be a later version.

[38] Vielhauer and Strecker, 152ff.

[39] Matt 16:17–19; cf. 5:17–20.

[40] Matt 24:14; cf. 28:19.

[41] Reginald H. Fuller, "Matthew," in *Harper's Bible Commentary*, ed. James L. Mays (San Francisco: Harper and Row, 1988), 951.

[42] This remains a tension for modern Jewish Christians, who recognize Jesus as Messiah and consider themselves part of the church, but do not believe that they have ceased to be Jews.

II. Primitive Church Documents

While the work of Jean Danielou in the area of Jewish Christian theology is open to some criticism in terms of definition and methodology,[43] it does provide some illuminating insights into the theological paradigms of the primitive church. Danielou defined Jewish Christianity as Christian thought expressing itself in forms borrowed from Judaism.[44] By examining extant documents from the primitive church, he was able to learn much general information about early Jewish Christian theological concepts. While the limitations of this study do not permit a complete review of Danielou's work, a few of his findings provide useful background information.

Clearly, Danielou's definition of Jewish Christianity would have included the early Christian community in Jerusalem. Dominated by James, the brother of Jesus, and composed primarily of ethnic Jews, it was orthodox in its Christian doctrine but continued to follow a predominantly Jewish lifestyle. The Jerusalem community held the most prominent position in the primitive church until the fall of Jerusalem in 70 CE and the expulsion of that community from the city. Danielou believes that the Jewish Christians encountered in the second century by Justin and referred to by patristic authors as the "Nazarenes" are the descendants of this community.[45]

However, even as the stature of the predominantly Jewish Jerusalem community diminished and such predominantly Gentile Christian communities as Rome, Alexandria, and Antioch began to gain prominence in the late first and early second centuries, Jewish ideas and concepts continued to have a strong influence on Christian thinking. In fact, Danielou found that the primitive church was so extremely dependent on Jewish theological concepts that it is impossible to define the term Jewish Christian in any way that distinguishes it from the term Christian.[46] So while Christianity had

---

[43] Lüdemann, 29.

[44] Danielou, *Development*, 9.

[45] Danielou, *Development*, 8–9.

[46] A. F. J. Klijn, "The Study of Jewish-Christianity," *New Testament* 20 (1973/74): 419–431.

spread across the entire Mediterranean basin by the end of the first century, and while it was composed primarily of Gentile Christian communities, it was not until later in the second century that these Gentile Christian communities began to reformulate their inherited Jewish Christian theology within the Hellenistic paradigms native to their culture.[47] While Danielou's approach may not be useful for focusing study on the doctrines and practices of specific groups, it is helpful in that it demonstrates that the Christian church in its earliest form was a Jewish Christian phenomenon. And even when the church had become predominantly ethnically Gentile, it remained theologically Jewish Christian for some time.

It would be incorrect, using either Danielou's definition or that offered by this study, to speak of early Jewish Christianity as a unified movement. The early writers identified a number of different groups within Jewish Christianity, each with distinctive characteristics, but considered them all related to some degree.[48] It is certainly understandable that Jewish Christianity would display a wide variety of theology and practice since the Judaism of the time—out of which it emerged—also displayed a wide variety of theology and practice. It must be assumed that Jewish Christians who emerged from the party of the Pharisees would express their theological ideas in ways related to the theological paradigms of the Pharisees, whether consistent with or in reaction to those ideas.

---

[47] Danielou, *Development*, 9–10. According to Danielou, Christianity remained a "Judaistic religion" through the middle of the second century. The church remained "Judaistic" in three ways. First, the church continued to use the Hebrew Scriptures, which remained an indispensable part of the Christian heritage. Second, the earliest church borrowed from the thought-forms of the expressions of Judaism which existed at the time (e.g., Pharisaic, Essenism, and Zealotism) in order to express its theology. Third, the church remained engaged in continuous and open dispute with the "rabbinical, legalistic Judaism" which developed after the fall of Jerusalem. Judaism remained an active influence on Christianity through the fourth century. The Haggadic literature continued to influence Christian writers. Apologetic and patristic authors such as Justin, Origen, and Eusebius were in contact with Jews and Jewish literature: Justin was in contact with Trypho the Jew; Origen consulted rabbis for exegetical advice; and Eusebius was strongly influenced by the Haggadic literature. However, these were now minor parts of a whole that had ceased to have an authentically Jewish character.

[48] Klijn and Reinink, *PE*, (1973), ix.

Similarly, Jewish Christians who emerged from the Essene party would be expected to show the influence of the theological paradigms of that group. And both of the above would differ from the theological expressions of Jewish Christians emerging from the Zealot party. In fact, Danielou suggests this is exactly the case.

> Thus we find Palestinian Jewish Christians of a somewhat Pharisaic and legalistic tendency; apocalyptic and messianist groups in Asia Minor with Zealot characteristics; Christians under Essene influence, responsible at Rome for the *Shepherd of Hermas*, and at Edessa for *Odes to Solomon* and even a rabbinical type in the Aramaic-speaking churches of eastern Syria.[49]

It is clear that the diversity within first-century Jewish Christianity does, in fact, parallel the diversity within first-century Judaism.

---

[49] Danielou, *Development*, 10; cf. Acts 15:4–5, which refer to believers who were members of the party of the Pharisees.

2

Who Were the Jewish Christians? Examination of the Candidates Suggested by the Church Fathers

The following chapter will review the different groups identified by the church fathers as Jewish Christian. It will attempt to determine which of these groups likely actually existed and which fit this study's
definition of Jewish Christianity. It will also attempt to provide some insights
into the origin, composition, and theologies of those groups.

The church fathers identified several groups as being Jewish Christian. Some groups they merely named. However, as Klijn and Reinink point out, the church fathers provide significant information about five distinct groups: Cerinthians, Ebionites, Nazarenes, Symmachians, and Elkesaites.[50] In evaluating the data provided by the church fathers about Jewish Christians, the reader must bear in mind that in all of these cases the church fathers were writing against Jewish Christianity in order to prove it a heresy and to declare specific Jewish Christian groups heretical. In some cases, they were justifying the determination made by earlier writers. Other patristic authors were known to have a tendency to fabricate groups of followers around single known heretics; invent heresiarchs from group names; or contrive links between groups (e.g., one descending from another), in order to show a progression of heresy.[51] Therefore the patristic information must be evaluated closely.

---

[50] Klijn and Reinink, *PE*, ix.
[51] W. Brandt, *Elchasai, ein Religionstifter und sein Werk*, quoted in Pritz, *Nazarene*, 37. Epiphanius was especially known for this tendency.

I. Cerinthians

The Cerinthians are one of several Jewish Christian groups described by the church fathers as heretical. References to the Cerinthians are found in the writings of Irenaeus, Hippolytus, Pseudo-Tertullian, Eusebius, Epiphanius, and Jerome.

The earliest reference to the Cerinthians is by Irenaeus around 190 CE in his work *adversus haeresium*.[52] He refers to a "certain Cerinthus," a Jewish Christian heretic[53] teaching in Asia Minor and proclaiming that the world was not created by the "supreme God" but by an angel. Cerinthus claimed that Jesus was not born of a virgin and that he was merely a very righteous and wise human. Jesus and Christ were two separate entities. Christ was evidently some form of spiritual entity—descended on Jesus in the form of a dove after baptism. Then Jesus Christ preached the Father and performed miracles. Christ left Jesus before his passion and death. Then God raised Jesus from the dead.[54] Later in the same document, Irenaeus included Cerinthus among those who believed that the "Creator" and the "Father" were two separate entities.[55] Irenaeus placed Cerinthus as a first-century contemporary and acquaintance of the Apostle John.[56] However, Irenaeus never specifically identified the Cerinthians as a Jewish Christian group.

A. Hippolytus

Hippolytus (225 CE) was the first of the patristic authors to characterize the Cerinthians as a Jewish Christian.[57] However, beyond this identification, Hippolytus added little to the information Irenaeus provided. He merely repeated Irenaeus's assertions with

---

[52] *adv. haer*, 1.26.1 (*PE*, 103).

[53] *adv. haer*, 1.26.1–2 (*PE*, 103ff). While Irenaeus does not explicitly call Cerinthus a Jewish Christian, he implies this by discussing him in the context of the Ebionites.

[54] *adv. haer*. 1.26.1 (*PE*, 103).

[55] *adv. haer*. 3.11.2 (*PE*, 105). This group would have included Marionettes and Gnostics, among others.

[56] *adv. haer*. 3.3.4 (*PE*, 105).

[57] *ref.* 7.79 (*PE*, 111).

some minor changes apparently designed to identify the Cerinthians more closely with Gnostics.[58]

B. Pseudo-Tertullian

Pseudo-Tertullian (ca. 200/250 CE) attempted to establish Cerinthus as the predecessor of Ebion.[59] However, many argue that this is doubtful, since most early Christian writers suggested direct linkages between similar heresies, whether or not they had solid evidence of such linkages.[60]

C. Eusebius

Eusebius (ca. 320 CE) also gives little new information, except to state that the Cerinthians existed at the same time as the Ebionites.[61]

D. Epiphanius

Epiphanius (ca. 376 CE) associates Cerinthus with Judaism, on the basis of his saying that the law and the prophets were given by angels.[62] Klijn and Reinink note that Epiphanius accused Cerinthus of causing confusion in the Church of Antioch by saying Gentiles should be circumcised,[63] turning the Jews in Jerusalem against Paul,[64] and being one of the "pseudo-apostles" described by Paul.[65] Epiphanius reconciled the apparent differences between Judaism and Cerinthian Gnosticism by claiming that Cerinthus's Gnostic doctrines were a later development.

Epiphanius noted that like the Ebionites, the Cerinthians used an edited Gospel of Matthew. However, unlike the Ebionites, who (as I will later show) removed Jesus's genealogies, the

---

[58] *ref.* 733.1–2 (*PE*, 111–112); 10.21.1–3 (*PE*, 121).

[59] *adv. omn. haer.* 3 (*PE*, 123).

[60] Pritz, *Nazarene*, 37.

[61] *hist. eccl.* 3.28.1 (*PE*, 141).

[62] Klijn and Reinink, *PE*, 9; cf. *pan.* 28.1.3 (*PE*, 163).

[63] Klijn and Reinink, *PE*, 9; cf. *pan.* 28.2.3 (*PE*, 163); Acts 14:24.

[64] Klijn and Reinink, *PE*, 9; cf. *pan.* 28.4.1 (*PE*, 165); Acts 21:28.

[65] Klijn and Reinink, *PE*, 9; cf. *pan.* 28.4.1–2 (*PE*, 165); 2 Cor 11:13.

Cerinthians did not remove Jesus's genealogy because they believed that it proved Jesus was the son of Joseph and Mary.[66] They believed that Christ had not yet been raised but would rise with the general resurrection.[67] In addition, they rejected the authority of the Apostle Paul.[68]

Apparently, Epiphanius had little direct knowledge of the Cerinthians. Nevertheless, he appears to have attached to them a number of heretical ideas which were prevalent in Asia Minor.[69]

E. Jerome

Jerome, writing in the late fourth and early fifth centuries, mentions the Cerinthians briefly[70] but appears to know nothing beyond an association with Ebion.

Beyond establishing the fact that Cerinthus was a first-century Jewish Christian heretic in Asia Minor, there seems to be little of historical value for the study of Jewish Christianity in the early Christian writings. The earliest writers seemed to know of no group by the name, but only Cerinthus himself. The information describing Cerinthian beliefs is contradictory. Klijn and Reinink argue that most of the claims advanced by the church fathers in regard to the Corinthians as a group appear to be mere speculations.[71]

II. Ebionites

Another group described as Jewish Christian by the church fathers was the Ebionites. The Ebionites are mentioned by the church fathers more frequently than any other group. Patristic information on the Ebionites comes from the following authors: Irenaeus,

---

[66] Klijn and Reinink, *PE*, 10; cf. *pan.* 30.14.2 (*PE,* 181).

[67] *pan.* 28.6.1 (*PE*, 165–166).

[68] *pan.* 28.5.3 (*PE*, 165).

[69] Klijn and Reinink, *PE*, 12.

[70] *adv. Luc.* 23 (*PE*, 203); *epist.* 112.13 (*PE*, 201); *in Matth.; praef.* (*PE*, 215); *de vir. ill.* 9 (*PE*, 211).

[71] Klijn and Reinink, *PE*, 19.

Tertullian, Hippolytus, Origen, Eusebius, Epiphanius, and Jerome, as well as other, non-contemporary writers.

The first written reports specifically mentioning the sect of Ebionites were written by Irenaeus (ca. 190 CE). Irenaeus compared the Ebionites to the Cerinthians, noting that the Ebionites differed from the Cerinthians in their view of creation, holding that the world was created by God rather than by some secondary demiurge.[72] The Ebionites also believed that Jesus was merely the son of Joseph and Mary[73] rather than of the Holy Spirit and Mary. Therefore, Irenaeus concluded that the Ebionites could not be saved, because they did not believe that God became man in Jesus Christ, and they rejected the virgin birth.[74] The Ebionites used only the Gospel of Matthew.[75] They repudiated Paul as an apostate from the law.[76] From Irenaeus's comments, it would appear that the Ebionites celebrated the Eucharist with water rather than wine.[77] Finally, Irenaeus noted that the Ebionites practiced circumcision, persevered in the customs ground in the law, and practiced a Jewish way of life, even adoring Jerusalem as if it were the house of God.[78]

A. Tertullian

Tertullian (ca. 200 CE) was the first to suggest that a person named Ebion actually existed.[79] Tertullian suggested that John 1:14 ("and the Word became flesh and dwelt among us.") was written against Ebion.[80] Tertullian confirms that the Ebionites believed that Jesus was a mere man,[81] and that they rejected Jesus's virgin birth[82] as

---

[72] Klijn and Reinink, *PE*, 19; cf. *adv. haer.* 1.26.2 (*PE*, 103–104).

[73] Klijn and Reinink, *PE*, 20; cf. *adv. haer.* 3.21.1 (*PE*, 107).

[74] Klijn and Reinink, *PE*, 20; cf. *adv. haer.* 4.33.4 (*PE*, 107); 5.1.3 (*PE*, 107).

[75] *adv. haer.* 1.26.2 (*PE* 105); 3.11.7 (*PE*, 105f).

[76] *adv. haer.* 1.76.2 (*PE*, 105); 3.11.7 (*PE*, 105f).

[77] *adv. haer.* 5.1.3 (*PE*, 107).

[78] *adv. haer.* 1.26.2 (*PE*, 105).

[79] *de praesc.* 32.3–5 (*PE*, 107f); 33.11 (*PE*, 108).

[80] *de carne* 24 (*PE*, 111).

[81] *de carne* 14, 18 (*PE*, 109f); *de praesc.* 33.11 (*PE*, 109).

[82] *de virg. vel.* 6.1 (*PE*, 109).

well as his resurrection.[83] He also confirms that they defended circumcision and the law.[84]

B. Hippolytus

Hippolytus (225 CE) confined his remarks primarily to Ebionite theology and Christology. He also considered Ebion to be a real person[85] and restated previous writers' assertions that Ebionites believed that the world was made by the true God (as opposed to a lesser demiurge).[86] He adds that they believed that they were "justified according to the Law."[87] They believed Jesus was a man like others, justified by practicing the law, and was called the Christ because he was the only human to have ever kept the law perfectly. If any other had kept the law perfectly, he would have been the Christ. Therefore, they believed they also could become Christs.[88]

C. Origen

Origen mentioned the Ebionites in several documents written between 225 and 250 CE. He repeated assertions of earlier writers that the Ebionites rejected the virgin birth,[89] observed the law[90] and circumcision,[91] and rejected Paul.[92]

Origen was the first to note that the Ebionites observed Easter on the Jewish Passover as a way of imitating Christ,[93] and that they believed that Jesus was sent only to the lost sheep of

---

[83] *de praesc.* 32.3.5 5 (*PE,* 107f).

[84] *de praesc.* 33.3–5 (*PE,* 108).

[85] *ref.* 7.35.1–2 (*PE,* 113).

[86] *ref.* 7.34.1 (*PE,* 113).

[87] *ref.* 7.34.1 (*PE,* 113).

[88] *ref.* 7.34.1–2 (*PE,* 113). Note the similarity to the modern theology of the Church of Jesus Christ of Latter-day Saints (Mormon).

[89] *in epist. ad Titum* 3:11 (*PE,* 133); *hom. in Luc.* 17 (*PE,* 127).

[90] *in epist. ad Rom.* 3.11 (*PE,* 133); *c.* Celsum 2.1 (*PE,* 135); *in Matth.* 16.12 (*PE,* 129f).

[91] *hom. in Gen.* 3.5 (*PE,* 127).

[92] *hom in Jer.* 19.12 (*PE,* 127); *c. Celsum* 5.65 (*PE,* 135).

[93] *in Matth.* Ser. 79 (*PE,* 131).

Israel.[94] He described a *Gospel According to the Hebrews*, which was an edited form of the Gospel According to Matthew, and quotes from it several times in various documents.[95] However, it is not clear whether he was ascribing these texts to the Ebionites or to some other Jewish Christian sect. In fact, Klijn and Reinink argue that the *Gospel According to the Hebrews* quoted by Origen should not be ascribed to the Ebionites, as it contains ideas dissimilar to those of the Ebionites.[96] Elsewhere Origen notes that there were "two kinds of Ebionites, some confessing that Jesus was born of a virgin as we do and others who deny this but say that he was born like other people."[97] I will argue later that one of the "two kinds of Ebionites" mentioned by Origen are, in fact, Nazarenes, and that the texts quoted by Origen belong to their version of the *Gospel According to the Hebrews*.

In documents written between 321 and 323 CE, Eusebius provides some additional information on the Ebionites. According to Eusebius, the Ebionites lived in the village of Chooba (a.k.a. Kochaba), which was east of the Jordan.[98] Like Origen, he also refers to two groups of Ebionites, one heretical and one relatively orthodox. The first group believed that Jesus was a mere man, born of Joseph and Mary, justified by his observance of the law.[99] They believed that people could not be saved by faith alone but that salvation required observance of law.[100] They rejected Paul as an apostate from the law and did not accept his epistles.[101] They used only the *Gospel of the Hebrews* and little else.[102] They celebrated both the Jewish Sabbath and the Lord's Day.[103] According to Eusebius, the other, apparently more orthodox group of Ebionites

---

[94] *de princ.* 4.3.8 (*PE*, 125); cf. Matt 10:6.

[95] *in Joh.,* 2.12 (*PE*, 127); *in Matth.* 15.14 (*PE*, 129); cf. *hom. in Jer.* 15.4 (*PE*, 127).

[96] Klijn and Reinink, *PE*, 25.

[97] *c. Celsum.* 5.61 (*PE*, 135); cf. 5.65; *in Matth.* 16.12 (*PE.* 131).

[98] *onomas.* 172.1–3 (*PE.* 151).

[99] *hist. eccl.* 3.27.2 (*PE*, 141).

[100] *hist. eccl.* 327.2 (*PE,* 141).

[101] *hist. eccl.* 3.27.4 (*PE*, 141).

[102] *hist. eccl.* 3.27.4 (*PE*, 141).

[103] *hist. eccl.* 3.27.5 (*PE*, 141).

"avoided the absurdity of the former and did not deny that the Lord was born of a virgin and the Holy Spirit."[104]

Eusebius spoke of two gospels used among Jewish Christians. One of these was the aforementioned *Gospel of the Hebrews*.[105] The other gospel, which he does not name, was written in Syriac or Aramaic and used among Jews who believed in Christ, but not by any particular sect.[106]

Epiphanius (ca. 376 CE) provided new information on the origins of the Ebionites. According to Epiphanius, the Ebionites originated at the time of the destruction of Jerusalem.[107] "All those who believed in Christ (Jewish Christians) had generally come...to Pella of the Decapolis" where they became the Nazarenes (another Jewish Christian group which will be discussed below). Ebion joined the Nazarenes there but eventually moved to Kochaba.[108] Living in close proximity to the Nazarenes, the Ebionites had some interaction with them, the extent of which Epiphanius does not make clear.[109] According to Epiphanius, the Ebionites eventually settled in a number of areas, including Nabataea, Paneas, Moabitis, Kochaba, and Adraa. From there, they eventually moved to Asia, Rome, and Cyprus.[110]

As to Ebionite beliefs, Epiphanius repeated earlier writers' assertions that the Ebionites used an edited version of the Gospel According to Matthew which he said they called the *Gospel According to the Hebrews*,[111] but he provided more information about its contents. The Ebionites claimed that the Holy Spirit "entered into" Jesus at his baptism, indicating a potentially adoptionistic belief that Jesus did not become Christ until his baptism.[112] Epiphanius noted that their gospel also omitted the

---

[104] *hist. eccl.* 3.27.3 (*PE*, 141).

[105] *hist. eccl.* 3.25.5 (*PE*, 139).

[106] *Theo.* (*PE*, 149).

[107] *pan.* 30.2.7–9 (*PE*, 177).

[108] *pan.* 30.2.7–9 (*PE*, 177).

[109] *pan.* 30.2.9 (*PE*, 177).

[110] *pan.* 30.18.1 (*PE*, 187).

[111] *pan.* 30.3.7 (*PE*, 179).

[112] *pan.* 30.13.1 (*PE*, 181). This would not by itself constitute proof of adoptionistic beliefs. However, elsewhere Epiphanius indicates that the Ebionites believed that Jesus become the Christ through his work.

genealogy of Jesus, which Epiphanius interpreted as a rejection of virgin birth.[113]

The Ebionites apparently rejected the eating of meat since their gospel portrayed many major characters as vegetarians. John the Baptist rejects the eating of meat (e.g., locusts are omitted from his diet).[114] At the Last Supper, Jesus wonders if he should eat meat.[115] Peter was also described in this text as a vegetarian.[116]

In addition to the *Gospel of the Hebrews*, the Ebionites also used other books such as the "so-called *Periodi of Peter*, which were written by Clement, but they corrupted the contents leaving not much that is true."[117] This would indicate some association between the Ebionites and the writers of the Pseudo-Clementine literature, but the exact relationship is not clear.[118]

Epiphanius described Ebionite Christological beliefs as confused,[119] in large part because of the influence of Elxai (the purported leader of the Elkesaites, another group identified as Jewish Christian by the church fathers, to be discussed below).[120] Examples of Elxai's influence on Ebionite thinking included the following Christological conceptions:[121] (1) Adam was Christ; (2) Jesus was a man on whom Christ descended; and (3) Christ was a spirit, the first creation, the Lord of the angels, who entered into Adam and into the patriarchs, again assumed the form of Adam (Jesus), was crucified, and returned to heaven.[122] It was on the basis of such beliefs as the above that Epiphanius attempted to link the Ebionites to the Cerinthians. He noted that the Ebionites forbade the eating of meat.[123] He repeated earlier writers' contentions that the

---

[113] *pan.* 30.13.6 (*PE*, 181).
[114] *pan.* 30.14.4 (*PE*, 181).
[115] *pan.* 30.22.3–5 (*PE*, 189).
[116] *pan.* 15.1.3 (*PE*, 183).
[117] *pan.* 30.15.1 (*PE*, 183).
[118] Klijn and Reinink, *PE*, 31.
[119] *pan.* 30.3.1 (*PE*, 177).
[120] *pan.* 30.3.2 (*PE*, 177).
[121] *pan.* 30.3.5–6 (*PE*, 178).
[122] cf. *pan.* 30.14.2 (*PE*, 181); 30.16.3 (*PE*, 183); 30.18.5 (*PE*, 187).
[123] *pan.* 30.15.3 (*PE*, 183).

Ebionites adhered to Judaism, lived according to the law, kept the Sabbath, practiced circumcision,[124] and rejected Paul.[125]

The question must be raised as to the sources of Epiphanius's information regarding the Ebionites. Was it the result of firsthand knowledge of the sect, or did he obtain the information from other sources? If it was from other sources, were those sources contemporary? The answers to these questions cannot be established firmly. Many researchers believe that Epiphanius did not have firsthand contact with the Ebionites[126] and that most of what he wrote about the Ebionites he drew from written sources.[127] Epiphanius appears to have drawn in large part on the works of Irenaeus and Hippolytus,[128] dating from about 190 CE and 225 CE, respectively.[129] Another was the so-called *Gospel of the Ebionites*, along with some other Ebionite materials, which may or may not have been contemporaneous.[130] On the other hand, some of Epiphanius's material—information which appears to have been current in the Jewish Christian communities of his day—appears to have passed to him orally.[131] In addition, during portions of his life he was in a position to come into contact with Jewish Christians and others who might have had firsthand knowledge of Ebionites. Epiphanius was born in Judea and lived and traveled in the Middle East for many years, finally moving to Rome in 382 CE. His native tongue was Syrian, and he also had some knowledge of Hebrew.[132] He spoke of the Ebionites in the present tense as though they still existed, making it possible, though not certain, that they did.

---

[124] *pan.* 30.2.2 (*PE*, 175f).
[125] *pan.* 30.16.8–9 (*PE*, 185).
[126] Klijn and Reinink, *PE*, 38; Pritz, *Nazarene,* 30.
[127] Klijn and Reinink, *PE*, 38; Pritz, *Nazarene,* 30.
[128] Klijn and Reinink, *PE*, 34; Pritz, *Nazarene,* 30.
[129] Klijn and Reinink, *PE*, 103, 110.
[130] Klijn and Reinink, *PE*, 34.
[131] Klijn and Reinink, *PE,* 38.
[132] Pritz, *Nazarene,* 29.

D. Jerome

Jerome added nothing to what earlier writers had stated about the Ebionites. He spoke of them only in the most general terms and appeared to know no clear distinction between the Ebionites and the Nazarenes.[133]

E. Conclusions

The largely coherent portrait of the Ebionites provided by the church fathers establishes the existence of the Ebionites (and perhaps some related groups) from as early as the middle of the first century to perhaps as late as the end of the fourth century. They were apparently a law-observant Jewish Christian group which held heretical Christological beliefs and which rejected the authority of the Apostle Paul and most of the Scriptures. In addition, Epiphanius connects them with the writers of the *Pseudo-Clementines*, a connection accepted by most researchers.[134]

The application of the term Ebionite to all Jewish Christians, as seen in Origen, Eusebius, and Epiphanius, was typical of the confusion and ambivalence of the orthodox church regarding Jewish Christianity and of the previously mentioned tendency of the church fathers, especially Epiphanius, to fabricate links between similar heresies. According to Origen and Eusebius, there were two kinds of Ebionites, one of which apparently was relatively orthodox. I will argue below that based on their descriptions of the theology and Christology of this second kind of "Ebionite," Origen and Eusebius may have mistakenly labeled as Ebionite a separate and distinct group of Jewish Christians known as the Nazarenes.

III. Nazarenes

The Nazarenes were not named in the patristic literature until 374 CE, when Epiphanius mentioned them in the *Anacortus*[135] and later

---

[133] *epist.* 112.13 (*PE*, 201).
[134] Klijn and Reinink, *PE*, 31f.
[135] *anacor.* 13.3 (*PE*, 155).

(ca. 276 CE) described them in the Panarion. However, although the earlier writers Origen and Eusebius had not mentioned the Nazarenes by name, they did describe a second kind of "Ebionite" group: a more orthodox group with Christology and practices close to what Epiphanius attributed to the Nazarenes. Justin Martyr, writing even earlier, mentions neither Ebionites nor Nazarenes by name, but does describe two Jewish Christian factions similar to them.

A. Justin Martyr

In his *Dialogue with Trypho the Jew*, written after 150 CE, Justin refers to Jewish Christians, or as he calls them, "those who wish to observe such institutions as were given by Moses ... along with their hope in Christ ... yet choose to live with the Christians and the faithful." He allows that Jewish Christians may practice the ceremonial law without detriment to their salvation as long as they do not attempt to convince Gentile converts that they must follow the law.[136] At the same time, he also condemns those who do not accept Christ's divinity.[137] Justin's use of the present tense in these comments shows that by the middle of the second century there were still Jewish Christians of at least two sorts, at least one of which was relatively orthodox by Justin's standards. Clearly, Jewish Christians were active in evangelistic efforts, even among the Gentiles. Some attempted to persuade Gentiles to keep the law, while others did not. Also, some denied the virgin birth of Jesus, while others appeared to vary from orthodoxy only in their keeping of the law. For Justin, following the ceremonial law was only a danger if it led a person to return to normative Judaism and reject Jesus as the Messiah.[138] Justin saw following the Jewish rituals as ineffective, but not sinful or heretical. While acknowledging that some of his contemporaries condemned such people, Justin holds that "we ought to join ourselves to such, and associate with them in all things as kinsmen and brethren."[139]

---

[136] *Dial.* 47.1f, in Pritz, *Nazarene*, 20.
[137] *Dial.* 48, in Pritz, *Nazarene*, 20.
[138] *Dial.* 47.4ff, in Pritz, *Nazarene*, 20.
[139] *Dial.* 47, in Pritz, *Nazarene*, 20.

B. Origen

Writing around 250 CE, Origen observed two different kinds of Ebionites, describing them as follows:

> Let it be admitted, moreover, that there are some [Jews] who accept Jesus, and who boast on that account of being Christians, and yet would regulate their lives, like the Jewish multitudes, in accordance with the Jewish law, and these are the twofold sect of the Ebionites, who either acknowledge with us that Jesus was born of a virgin, or deny this, and maintain that he was begotten like other human beings.[140]

Origen's description again reveals two types of "Ebionites": one which denied Jesus's divinity; and another which held to the orthodox position regarding Christ's divinity. Some suggest that the latter group of Ebionites may not be Ebionites at all but a separate and distinct Jewish Christian group called "Nazarenes."[141] This suggestion is supported by the fact that the beliefs described above are consistent with those later attributed to the Nazarenes by Epiphanius. In other texts, Origen seems to be confusing the two groups. Observing that the Ebionites self-described motivation for observing the law was to be "imitators of Christ," he notes that this is inconsistent with their heretical beliefs.[142] In fact, such a motivation would be more consistent with Nazarene beliefs than with those of the Ebionites.[143] In any case, one can see in the above texts the beginnings of a tendency to lump together and confuse different law-observant Jewish Christian sects under the catchall

---

[140] c. Celsum 5.61 (PE, 135).

[141] Pritz, Nazarene, 21.

[142] Origen, in Matth. Ser 79 (PE, 131).

[143] Epiphanius, pan. 29.7.2 (PE, 173); cf. 1 Cor 11; Eph 5:1; 1 Thess 1:6. As described below, Epiphanius noted that the Nazarenes accepted the letters of the Apostle Paul, while the Ebionites rejected them. Therefore, it seems unlikely that the Ebionites would have used such a characteristically Pauline phase as "imitators of Christ." The most likely explanation is that Origen has confused the two groups and mistakenly attributed this motivation to the Ebionites.

term Ebionite, a tendency which would only grow more pronounced over time.[144]

Writing in 324 CE, Eusebius again noted two kinds of Ebionites. One group held Christ "to be a plain and ordinary man who had achieved righteousness merely by the progress of his character and had been born naturally from Mary and her husband."[145] This group "insisted on the complete observation of the law and did not think that they would be saved by faith in Christ."[146] The other group "did not deny that the Lord was born of a virgin and the Holy Spirit."[147]

Eusebius was the first to describe the departure of Jewish Christians from Jerusalem to Pella of Perea (in the area known as the Decapolis), after being warned by a revelation about its coming destruction.[148] Presumably, Eusebius thought this group to be orthodox at the time of their departure from Jerusalem since he speaks of them as "people of the Church" of Jerusalem who "believed in Christ." In addition, Klijn and Reinink argue that none of the church fathers of the time would have allowed that heretics might receive a revelation from God.[149] Eusebius's comments certainly establish that at least two groups of Jewish Christians continued to exist in his time. If the second of these groups is taken to be the Nazarenes, as the idea suggests, and as many researchers believe, then Eusebius documents the existence of the Nazarenes into at least the early fourth century.[150]

The first and most extensive description of the Nazarenes by name was written by Epiphanius in the *Panarion* (a.k.a. *adversus haereses* or *Against Heresies*), which was written about 376 CE. Epiphanius gives several pieces of information about a group of people who call themselves the Nazarenes, although he notes that

---

[144] Pritz, *Nazarene*, 21.

[145] *hist. eccl.* 3.27.2 (*PE,* 141).

[146] *hist. eccl.* 3.27.2 (*PE,* 141).

[147] *hist. eccl.* 3.27.3 (*PE,* 141).

[148] *hist. eccl.* 3.5.3 (*PE,* 141).

[149] Klijn and Reinink, *PE*, 45.

[150] Pritz, *Nazarene,* 28; Joseph A. Fitzmyer, "The Qumran Scrolls, the Ebionites and Their Literature," *Theological Studies* 16(3), (1955): 341–342.

"all Christians were called Nazarenes once."[151] The Nazarenes existed from the earliest days of Christianity.[152] They had their origin from the Jerusalem congregation of Jewish disciples which fled to Pella of the Decapolis before 70 CE, guided by a revelation of Christ which warned them of its coming siege. (He considered them to be still orthodox at the time of their departure.[153]) Some had already left Jerusalem following Jesus' ascension and were called Iessaeans for a short period of time.[154] He also noted that their geographic location in Pella placed them in close proximity to the Ebionites.[155] (This close geographic proximity might explain why the two groups were frequently confused by patristic writers.) By the year 129 CE, according to Epiphanius, the Nazarenes (or at least a significant number of them) returned to Jerusalem, where they "performed great signs," and because of them others were "prodded" in their minds and "believed in Christianity."[156] Their evangelistic activities were directed towards their Jewish brothers and sisters in the synagogues, and this created a great deal of animosity toward them among the Jewish leadership. Epiphanius noted that they were hated by the Jews and cursed in the synagogues three times a day.[157] By Epiphanius's time they had settled in the areas of Pella, Kochaba, and Coele in Syria.[158]

Epiphanius attempted to make a connection between the Nazarenes and both the Elkesaites and the Ebionites. He claimed that the Nazarenes were joined by Elxai and later adopted his book.[159] He also claimed that Ebion came out of them.[160] These last

---

[151] *pan.* 29.1.3 (*PE,* 169).

[152] *pan.* 29.1.1 (*PE,* 169).

[153] *pan.* 29.7.8 (*PE,* 173); cf. *hist. eccl.* 3.5.3 (*PE,* 139); Klijn and Reinink, *PE,* 45. As mentioned previously, Klijn and Reinink argue that Epiphanius would not have allowed that heretics would have received a revelation and certainly not a revelation from Christ.

[154] *pan.* 29.5.4 (*PE,* 169).

[155] *pan.* 30.2.8 (*PE,* 177).

[156] *Weights* 14–15, in Craig Koester, "The Origin and Significance of the Flight to Pella Tradition," *Catholic Bible Quarterly* 51(1989): 93.

[157] *pan.* 29.9.2–3 (*PE,* 173ff).

[158] *pan.* 29.7.7 (*PE,* 173).

[159] *pan.* 19.1.4 (*PE,* 155); 19.4.1. (*PE,* 161); cf. 53.1.3 (*PE,* 195).

[160] *pan.* 30.2.1 (*PE,* 175).

statements are problematic. There is considerable doubt among scholars whether an actual person named Elxai ever existed, or whether there was only a *Book of Elxai* (Heb. for "hidden power") and he was merely a convenient creation.[161] There is near unanimous agreement among scholars that the Christology of the Nazarenes was so different from that of the Elkesaites that it would have been unlikely that the Nazarenes would ever have adopted the *Book of Elxai*.[162] Elkesaite Christology was more Pythagorean in nature, including concepts (e.g., reincarnation) foreign to the Nazarenes.[163] Epiphanius was known for his attempts to develop a line of succession from heresy to heresy, with each outdoing the last. Hence, he may have been trying in this case to lump Jewish Christian groups together despite the lack of evidence to support such a theory.[164]

There is also considerable doubt as to the historicity of a person named Ebion.[165] Irenaeus, who was the first to mention the Ebionites, appeared to know only the group name, which is Hebrew for "poor."[166] On the other hand, even if the person of Ebion may not be historical, it is likely that the comment that "Ebion came out of them" does reflect an actual event. Pritz argues that at the time of the fall of Jerusalem, only one group of Jewish Christians left Jerusalem for Pella: the group which would eventually be called Nazarenes. In Pella, sometime in the second century, the Nazarenes suffered some schism in their number, probably over Christology, and the group that would become the Ebionites broke off from the Nazarenes and moved to a nearby village. If the Ebionites did break off from the Nazarenes and lived in close geographic proximity to them, this would tend to account for the church fathers' confusion between the two sects.[167]

---

[161] Pritz, *Nazarene*, 36.

[162] Pritz, *Nazarene*, 37.

[163] cf. Hippolytus, *refut. omn. haer.* 9.14.1 (*PE*, 117).

[164] Pritz, *Nazarene*, 37.

[165] Pritz, *Nazarene*, 37.

[166] *adv. haer.* 1.26.2 (*PE*, 105); 3.11.7 (*PE*, 105); 3.21.1 (*PE*, 107); 4.33.4 (*PE*, 107); 5.1.3 (*PE*, 107).

[167] Pritz, *Nazarene*, 38.

Epiphanius also commented on the beliefs of the Nazarenes. They observed the law of Moses, but differed from other Jews in that they accepted Christ.[168] They used both the Old Testament and the New Testament, including the writings of Paul.[169] They had a good knowledge of Hebrew and read the Old Testament and at least one Gospel (Matthew) in Hebrew.[170] Apparently, this gospel was a different version than the *Gospel According to the Hebrews*, which was used by the Ebionites, in that Epiphanius is unaware of any heretical notions contained in it.[171] They believed in one God, who was the Creator of all things, and his son Jesus Christ.[172] Epiphanius was uncertain whether the Nazarenes accepted the virgin birth of Jesus, because he did not know whether their gospel contained Jesus's genealogy.[173] They did believe in the resurrection of the dead.[174]

It is important to ask how much credibility can be given to Epiphanius's accounts of the Nazarenes. Epiphanius was known for constructing links between heretical sects where no such links existed.[175] Indeed, most of Epiphanius's links between Jewish Christian groups have been discounted above. The proposed split-off of the Ebionites from the Nazarenes appears to be the only likely historical link. Epiphanius was also known for citing only evidence which supported his own viewpoints.[176] However, in this case, since Epiphanius's intentions were to declare the Nazarenes heretical solely based on their observance of the ceremonial law, one would have to give more credence to Epiphanius's observations of an otherwise orthodox theology, since such observations would not tend to advance his case. Finally, most researchers believe that Epiphanius had little direct contact with the Nazarenes, deriving most of his information from secondary sources.[177] However, at

---

[168] *pan.* 29.7.5 (*PE,* 173).
[169] *pan.* 29.7.2 (*PE,* 173).
[170] *pan.* 29.7.4 (*PE,* 173); 29.9.4 (*PE,* 175).
[171] *pan.* 29.9.4 (*PE,* 175).
[172] *pan.* 29.7.3–4 (*PE,* 173).
[173] *pan.* 29.7.6 (*PE,* 173); cf. 29.9.4 (*PE,* 175).
[174] *pan.* 29.7.4 (*PE,* 173).
[175] Pritz, *Nazarene,* 29.
[176] Pritz, *Nazarene,* 39.
[177] Pritz, *Nazarene,* 39.

several times in his life Epiphanius was in a position to come into contact with people who would have been in contact with the Nazarenes, having been born in Judea and having traveled in the Middle East.[178] Indeed, Pritz argues that some of Epiphanius's knowledge would have been much more likely to come from Nazarene or Ebionite sources than from secondary documents within the greater church.[179]

C. Filaster

Filaster was notable more for what he did not say about the Nazarenes than for what he did say. A contemporary of Epiphanius, he wrote an extensive compendium of heretical groups in about 385 CE which conspicuously omitted the Nazarenes.[180] This suggests that Filaster did not agree that the Nazarenes were heretical or else was unaware of them. In either case, it would seem that up until the time of Epiphanius the Nazarenes were orthodox enough to escape the notice of the heresiologists and that Epiphanius took it upon himself to include them in his own list of heresies.[181]

D. Jerome

It is possible that Jerome may have at least had contact with individuals who themselves were in direct contact with the Nazarenes. Writing in 392 CE, he claimed to have seen and received permission to make a copy of their Gospel of Matthew, which was written in "Hebrew letters."[182] Elsewhere he called this same text the *Gospel According to the Hebrews* and noted that it was written

---

[178] Pritz, *Nazarene*, 29.
[179] Pritz, *Nazarene*, 38.
[180] Pritz, *Nazarene*, 71; cf. *div. haer. liber.* 36, 37, 50, 57 (*PE*, 233). Filaster mentions the Cerinthians, the Ebionites, and the Symmachians, but not the Nazarenes. Pritz argues that this omission is especially significant since Filaster was so rigid in his orthodoxy that he condemned even those groups which disagreed with the Church on the fixed positions of the stars in the heavens.
[181] Pritz, *Nazarene*, 75.
[182] *de vir. ill.* 3 (*PE*, 211).

in Syriac (Aramaic).[183] However, it is obviously different from the gospel of the same name used by the Ebionites, containing none of the heretical ideas of the Ebionite version.[184] Klijn and Reinink note that if this was the same gospel to which Hegesippus referred, then the Nazarenes must have originated among Palestinian Jewish Christians at a very early date.[185] If Jerome's claim to have seen and copied the Nazarene Gospel were true, he would have to have done this during the several years that he resided in the wilderness of Chalcis ad Belum near Berea starting around 375 CE.[186] Jerome listed Berea as a home for some of the Nazarenes, but noted that they could also be found "in all the synagogues of the East among the Jews."[187] Living near Berea, Jerome would have been well situated to learn about them by interacting with those who did have a firsthand knowledge of them.[188] Klijn and Reinink note that Jerome records that he was taught Hebrew by a Jewish Christian during those years in the desert, and it is possible that this person could have been from Berea.[189] On the other hand, they argue that Jerome contradicted himself on a major Christological point in two separate descriptions of the Nazarenes and they suggest that this raises doubts about his claims of personal contact with the Nazarenes.[190] Pritz, while arguing convincingly against Klijn and Reinink's contention that the two texts in question are contradictory, nonetheless agrees with their assertion that he was unlikely to have

---

[183] *adv. Paleg.* 3.2 (*PE*, 227f).

[184] *adv. Paleg.* 3.2 (*PE*, 227).

[185] Klijn and Reinink, *PE*, 50.

[186] Pritz, *Nazarene*, 49; Klijn and Reinink, 47. Pritz argues for a two-year period starting in 375 CE. Klijn and Reinink argue for a five-year period starting in 374 CE.

[187] *de. vir. ill.* 3 (*PE*, 211).

[188] Pritz, *Nazarene,* 51.

[189] Klijn and Reinink, *PE*, 47; cf. *epist.* 125.12.1 (*PE*, 203).

[190] Klijn and Reinink, *PE*, 47; cf. *in Matth.* 13.53–54 (*PE*, 217); *epist.* 112.13 (*PE*, 201), Klijn and Reinink suggest that in the first document, written in 398 CE, Jerome implied that the Nazarenes rejected the virgin birth ("Strange stupidity of the Nazarenes! They wonder whence wisdom possessed wisdom and power possessed powers, but their obvious error is that they looked only on the son of the carpenter."). However, in the second text, written in 404 CE, Jerome clearly stated that they accepted the virgin birth.

had direct personal contact with the Nazarenes.[191] Still, the fact that Jerome writes of the Nazarenes in the present tense and was well placed to interact with those who were in contact with them indicates that they may well have remained in existence through at least the end of the fourth century or the beginning of the fifth.[192]

Commenting on the beliefs of the Nazarenes, Jerome recorded that they used both the Old Testament and the New Testament, including the writings of Paul.[193] They accepted Paul as an apostle, as well as his mission to the Gentiles, and did not believe that obedience to the law was required of them.[194] In 404 CE he wrote that "they believe in Christ, the Son of God, born of Mary the Virgin, and they say about him that he suffered under Pontius Pilate and rose again" (note the similarities to the Nicene creedal formulation).[195] Discussing their commentary on Isaiah, Jerome cited "this passage from the Gospel read by the Nazarenes, which was written in the Hebrew language: 'The whole fountain of the Holy Spirit came upon him' (Jesus) at his baptism."[196] He recorded that they observed the law,[197] that they had a gospel in Hebrew,[198] and that they accepted apostolic authority and called their Jewish brethren to "turn to him [Christ] and his Apostles."[199]

---

[191] Pritz, *Nazarene,* 54; cf. *in Matth.* 13.53–54 (*PE,* 217); *epist.* 112.13 (*PE,* 201). Fritz argues that Jerome's comments about the Nazarene error of looking "only at the son of the carpenter" is not a reference to Nazarene Christology. Rather, he argues that it is Jerome's commentary on Matt 13:53–58 in which Jesus returns to his own country (Nazareth) and is rejected by the people there. In other words, Jerome is using the term Nazarenes to refer to the people of the town of Nazareth.

[192] Pritz, *Nazarene,* 51.

[193] *in Esaiam* 9.1 (*PE,* 223).

[194] *in Esaiam* 9.1 (*PE,* 223).

[195] *epist.* 112.13 (*PE,* 201).

[196] *in Esaiam* 11.1–3 (*PE,* 223). The precise meaning of the term "fountain" is unclear but does demonstrate at least a primitive concept of the Holy Spirit.

[197] *in Esaiam* 8.11–15 (*PE,* 221); *in Hiez.* 16.16 (*PE,* 227); *in Hiez.* 3.14–16 (*PE,* 229).

[198] *de vir. ill.* 3 (*PE,* 211); *in Matth.* 12.13 (*PE,* 217); *in Esaiam* 11.1–3 (*PE,* 223); 40.9–11 (*PE,* 225); *prol.* 65 (*PE,* 227); *adv. Pelag.* 3.2 (*PE,* 227f); *in Hiez.* 18:5–9 (*PE,* 227).

[199] *in Esaiam* 31.6–9 (*PE,* 223f).

Jerome also provided information on the Nazarenes' relationship with the developing communities of rabbinic Judaism. Citing passages from the Nazarene commentary on Isaiah, he noted that they were cursed in the synagogues.[200] The Nazarenes interpreted Isaiah 29:17–21 as a prophecy against the Scribes and Pharisees and accused the Scribes and Pharisees of making "men sin against the Word of God in order that they should deny the Son of God."[201] On Isaiah 31:6–9, Jerome writes: "The Nazarenes understand this passage in this way: O sons of Israel, who deny the Son of God with such hurtful resolution."[202] They rejected the authority of Pharisaic scholars to interpret scripture definitively.[203] They rejected the Mishnah (oral tradition) as binding on themselves or any Jew.[204] Also, on Isaiah 8:14, he notes their condemnation of Shammai and Hillel, and those who followed after them, including Akiba.[205] This indicates continuing contact between the Nazarenes and the formative communities of rabbinic Judaism through at least the middle of the second century.

Jerome's comments on the Nazarenes described a Jewish Christian group which was apparently orthodox in their beliefs yet followed the law. This group had originated in the first-century church and was apparently still in existence in Jerome's time.

---

[200] *epist.* 112.13 (*PE*, 201); *in Amos* 1.11–12 (*PE*, 219); *in Esaiam* 5.18–19 (*PE*, 221); 49.7 (*PE*, 225); 52.4–6 (*PE*, 225); *in Hiez.* 16.13 (*PE*, 227).

[201] *in Esaiam* 29.17–21 (*PE*, 223).

[202] *in Esaiam* 31.6–9 (*PE*, 223).

[203] *in Esaiam* 8.14 (*PE*, 221).

[204] *in Esaiam* 8.14 (*PE*, 221), cf. Raymond A. Pritz, "The Jewish Christian Sect of the Nazarenes and the Mishnah," in *Proceedings of the Eighth World Congress of Jewish Studies, Division A–The Period of the Bible* (Jerusalem, Israel: Magnes Press, 1981), 125–130.

[205] *in Esaiam* 8.14 (*PE*, 221); cf. Justin, *Apol.* 31, quoted in Pritz, *Nazarene Jewish Christianity,* 59; Eusebius, *chron.* 283, quoted in Pritz, 59. It should be noted that it was Rabbi Akiba's proclamation of a false Messiah— Simon ben Cosiba (Bar Kochba), which led to the final split between Jewish Christianity and rabbinic Judaism.

E. Augustine

While Augustine provided no new information (Augustine appears to have depended entirely upon Epiphanius), his endorsement of Epiphanius's judgment that the Nazarenes were heretical seemed to have had a major influence on those church writers which followed him, reflecting the Nazarenes' final rejection by the church.[206] All of Augustine's references to the Nazarenes were negative.[207] He never quoted from their gospel and apparently had no personal contact with them.[208] However, it seems clear from the way in which Augustine described the Nazarenes that he considered them to be a currently existing Jewish Christian group:

> And now, certain heretics exist who call themselves Nazarenes, who, however, by some people are named Symmachians and who practice the circumcision of the Jews and the baptism of the Christians.[209]

These remarks, recorded by Augustine around 405–406 CE, establish the likelihood that the Nazarenes continued in existence into the fifth century.[210]

F. Conclusions

The evidence provided by the church fathers appears to demonstrate that the Nazarenes, a Jewish Christian group—orthodox in all respects except for their practice of the ceremonial law—existed as a distinct group from the time of the fall of Jerusalem until the late fourth or early fifth century. They were descendants of the Jewish Christian church in Jerusalem, which escaped to Pella after the fall of Jerusalem. They recognized the authority of the Apostle Paul and his mission to the Gentiles as well as the authority of the greater

---

[206] Pritz, *Nazarene,* 76.

[207] Pritz, *Nazarene,* 76.

[208] Pritz, *Nazarene,* 77.

[209] *c. Cres.* 1.31.36.

[210] Klijn and Reinink, 238; cf. *in Heiz,* 9 (*PE,* 238f). Augustine continued to write about the Nazarenes in the present tense as late as 428 CE.

church, of which they considered themselves a part. They evangelized their Jewish brethren in the synagogues. They accepted the entirety of the Scriptures, both the Old and New Testaments. They acknowledged that God was the Creator of all things and that Jesus Christ was the Son of God. They believed in the Holy Spirit. Epiphanius could find nothing to indicate that they denied Christ's virgin birth. They believed in the resurrection of the dead as well as Jesus's death and resurrection. They did follow the ceremonial law but did not believe it was essential for salvation. Rather, their motivation for following the ceremonial law was to be "imitators of Christ."[211] Up until the time of Epiphanius they apparently were sufficiently orthodox to escape the attention of the heresiologists. Apparently, it was solely on the basis of the Nazarenes' observance of the law that Epiphanius and all those who follow him determined that the Nazarenes were heretical.

IV. Symmachians

There is little information in the patristic literature about the Symmachians as a Jewish Christian group or Symmachus as a Jewish Christian. The information which is available is sketchy and most is inconsistent.

A. Origen

Origen mentions Symmachus in the context of an examination of variant translations of Zechariah 9:9 (Symmachus's translation read: "He was poor and sat upon a donkey and the colt of a she-donkey.")[212] Some suggest that Symmachus's choice of words in translating this verse suggest an Ebionite background. However, Klijn and Reinink consider this a very weak argument especially since Origen never actually referred to Symmachus as a Jewish Christian.[213]

---

[211] See footnote 143 in this chapter.
[212] in Matth. 16:16 (PE, 131).
[213] Klijn and Reinink, PE, 53.

B. Eusebius

Eusebius was the first writer to refer to Symmachus as an Ebionite Jewish Christian.[214] He noted that Symmachus's writings were still available at the time he was writing.[215] These included Symmachus's translation of the Hebrew Scriptures, which was widely used by the church fathers, as well as a commentary on the Gospel According to Matthew.[216]

C. Jerome

Jerome also classified Symmachus as an Ebionite.[217] He also agreed with Eusebius that Symmachus wrote a commentary on the Gospel According to Matthew.[218]

D. Ambrosiaster

Ambrosiaster was the first to refer to a group called the Symmachians.[219] He suggests that they are descendants of the Pharisees, who observe the law but call themselves Christians. Later writers also refer to the Symmachians as a group but many of the descriptions of the group are contradictory.[220]

E. Conclusions

There is little that can be made of this data. Apparently, Symmachus did exist and wrote a widely-used translation of the Old Testament. It seems likely he may have been Jewish Christian, if not an actual Ebionite. On the other hand, it seems unlikely that a group called the

---

[214] *hist. eccl.* 6.17 (*PE*, 147).

[215] *hist. eccl.* 6.17 (*PE*, 147).

[216] *hist. eccl.* 6.17 (*PE*, 147); cf. Klijn and Reinink, 53. It is unknown whether this was a complete or partial commentary.

[217] *in Hab.* 3.10–13 (*PE*, 209).

[218] *de vir. ill.* 54 (*PE*, 213).

[219] *ad Gal.* (*PE*, 197). Perhaps Symmachus himself emerged from descendants of the Pharisees.

[220] Klijn and Reinink, 54.

Symmachians existed, since the earliest Christian writers did not speak of such a group but only of the individual, Symmachus.[221]

V. Elkesaites

The Elkesaites are mentioned only by a few patristic authors. These authors are Hippolytus, Origen, and Epiphanius.

A. Hippolytus

Hippolytus (ca. 225 CE) was the first to mention the heretic Elxai. His information was given in several forms: descriptions of the preaching of Alcibiades, a reputed interpreter of Elxai;[222] descriptions of the contents of the *Book of Elxai*; and general doctrinal information. From the preaching of Alcibiades, Hippolytus described some of the beliefs of Elxai's followers, the Elkesaites. There was a special obligation of baptism for those who had misbehaved sexually.[223] All believers were required to be circumcised and to live according to the law.[224] Christ was born and reborn many times in the normal manner before being born of a virgin.[225] According to Hippolytus, they also adopted other Pythagorean ideas.[226] The *Book of Elxai* was said to be inspired by an angel of enormous size, who was the son of God, and a second female angel, who was the Holy Spirit.[227] According to Hippolytus's report on the *Book of Elxai*, the Elkesaites invoked seven spirits as witnesses during baptismal rites.[228] The Elkesaites conducted baptism but did so in the name of the "most high God."[229] Hippolytus also noted that they kept the Sabbath.[230] Otherwise, the contents of the book were similar to Alcibiades's preaching.

---

[221] Klijn and Reinink, *PE*, 53–54.

[222] *ref.* 9.17.2 (*PE*, 121).

[223] Klijn and Reinink, *PE*, 57; cf. *ref.* 9.13,4 (*PE*, 115).

[224] Klijn and Reinink, *PE*, 57; cf. *ref.* 9.4.1 (*PE*, 113f).

[225] Klijn and Reinink, *PE*, 56; cf. *ref.* 9.14.1 (*PE*, 117).

[226] Klijn and Reinink, *PE*, 56; cf. *ref.* 9.14.2 (*PE*, 117).

[227] *ref.* 9.13.2–3 (*PE*, 115).

[228] *ref.* 9.15.2 (*PE*, 117).

[229] *ref.* 9.15.1, 3 (*PE*, 117).

[230] *ref.* 9.16.3 (*PE*, 119).

B. Epiphanius

Epiphanius (ca. 376 CE) wrote both of a heretic named Elxai and of his followers the Elkesaites. According to Epiphanius, Elxai wrote a book supposedly inspired by divine wisdom and a prophecy.[231] He was of Jewish origin but had not lived according to the law.[232] As to the Elkesaites, as a group, Epiphanius noted (as did Hippolytus) that they venerated seven spirits or angels and invoked them as witnesses, especially during baptism.[233] They rejected virginity and chastity and were obliged to marry.[234] During the persecution they were allowed to worship idols.[235] They spoke of Jesus the Great King, though Epiphanius was unsure if they were actually referring to Jesus Christ.[236] They prayed in the direction of Jerusalem.[237] They rejected sacrifices and fire but venerated water.[238] They believed that Christ and the Holy Spirit were of enormous size.[239] They also maintained that Christ was "created first as Adam and reappears time and again...whenever he wished."[240] Finally, they rejected the eating of meat.[241]

C. Conclusions

The Elkesaites are of little importance for the study of Jewish Christianity. Klijn and Reinink argue that the *Book of Elxai* was most likely a product of an "apocalyptic-syncretistic, missionary movement which originated during the Roman invasion of Parthia within a Jewish community which tried to show its allegiance to the Parthians."[242] This seems likely, since the Elkesaites used the term

---

[231] *pan.* 19.1.4 (*PE*, 155).
[232] *pan.* 19.1.5 (*PE*, 155).
[233] *pan.* 19.1.6 (*PE*, 157).
[234] *pan.* 19.1.7 (*PE*, 157).
[235] *pan.* 19.2.1 (*PE*, 157).
[236] *pan.* 19.3.4 (*PE*, 157f).
[237] *pan.* 19.3.4 (*PE*, 157f).
[238] *pan.* 19.3.6–7 (*PE*, 159); cf. 53.1.7 (*PE*, 197).
[239] *pan.* 19.4.3–2 (*PE*, 159); 53.1.5–9 (*PE*, 197).
[240] *pan.* 53.1.8–9 (*PE*, 197).
[241] *pan.* 53.1–4 (*PE*, 195).
[242] Klijn and Reinink, *PE*, 66–67.

Christ (Messiah) without linking it to the person of Jesus, and when they did speak of Jesus the Great King, it was not clear if they were referring to Jesus Christ. Therefore, while the Elkesaites could not truly be called Jewish Christians, this does show that some Jewish Christian ideas were spreading throughout Jewish communities in the region and that they were influenced by a Christology like that of the *Pseudo-Clementines*, which must have existed prior to 200 CE.[243]

VI. Summary and Conclusions

This chapter's analysis of the comments of the church fathers regarding various Jewish Christian groups has provided additional focus to the investigation of Jewish Christianity in the early church. It has eliminated from consideration some of the groups which were traditionally but incorrectly classified as Jewish Christian groups. The Cerinthians can be eliminated because there is little evidence that such a group actually existed, although there is evidence that a Jewish Christian teacher named Cerinthus did exist. The Symmachians can be eliminated for the same reason. There was an individual Jewish Christian writer by the name of Symmachus who may have been an Ebionite. However, it is unlikely that a group called the Symmachians ever existed.

Although these individuals and groups must be eliminated from further study as Jewish Christian groups *per se,* their inclusion in the patristic record provides some insights into the attitude of the church fathers towards heresy generally and Jewish Christianity specifically. They demonstrate the tendency of some of the church fathers to "strengthen" their case against certain heresies by creating a following around an individual where no such following was likely to have existed;[244] creating an individual leader for a sect where no

---

[243] Klijn and Reinink, *PE*, 60.

[244] For example, the Cerinthians and the Symmachians were built up around Cerinthus and Symmachus, respectively.

such leader was likely to have existed;[245] or creating links between groups where no such links were likely to have existed.[246]

The elimination of the above groups leaves two named groups which can be considered Jewish Christian for the purposes of this study of the Nazarenes and the Ebionites. Both considered themselves to be Jewish; both considered themselves to be followers of Christ; both were actual historical groups. The Nazarenes were evidently the older of the two groups—being the direct descendants of the Jewish Christian community—which fled to Pella during the fall of Jerusalem. The Nazarenes were apparently orthodox in all ways except for the fact that they observed the law. Their theology was orthodox. Their Christology was orthodox. They accepted all of the canonical Scriptures as they were known at the time. They considered themselves a part of the greater church. They recognized apostolic authority, including that of the Apostle Paul and supported the law-free mission to the Gentiles while continuing to evangelize their brothers and sisters in the synagogues.[247] Their existence as a distinct group can be traced from the fall of Jerusalem until the late fourth or early fifth century. No patristic reports after that date describe them as a contemporary sect. Cut off from the greater church, they evidently faded from existence relatively quickly.

The Ebionites, on the other hand, were clearly a heretical group. Although they were a law-observant Jewish Christian group like the Nazarenes, they differed from them in many significant respects. They held heretical Christological beliefs (described above), rejected the authority of the Apostle Paul and his Gentile mission, and rejected most of the apostolic scriptures. They evidently split off from the Nazarenes sometime in the second century, possibly as a result of disagreements over Christology. Although they parted company with the Nazarenes, the Ebionites

---

[245] For example, Elxai was created for the Elkesaites. Epiphanius also created Ebion for the Ebionites.

[246] E.g., between the Cerinthians and the Ebionites, or between the Elkesaites and the Nazarenes.

[247] Perhaps the Nazarenes' acceptance of Paul's mission to the Gentiles, along with the Nazarenes' own evangelistic activity among their own brethren, reflects their memory of the agreement reached at the first Council of Jerusalem: Paul was to evangelize among the Gentiles and the Jerusalem church was to evangelize among the Jews.

continued to reside in the same general vicinity. Perhaps it was their common ancestry and the close proximity of the Ebionites and Nazarenes that led to the church fathers' tendency to confuse the two sects, using the term Ebionite to describe members not only of the Ebionite sect but of the Nazarene sect as well and eventually to use the term Ebionite as a synonym for Jewish Christianity, which the church fathers came to consider heretical. The reputation of the more orthodox Nazarenes no doubt suffered from this confusion with the heretical Ebionites. The tendency of the church fathers to confuse the Ebionites and the Nazarenes and to use the term Ebionite as catchall term for heretical Jewish Christian groups makes it likely that some groups classified by patristic authors as Ebionite were, in reality, other sects. For example, the groups described as Ebionites by Irenaeus and Origen are thought by some to be two (or three) different groups, separate from the Ebionites described by Epiphanius.[248] Others, including the author of this study, believe that Irenaeus and Origen, since they depict two types of "Ebionites"—one heretical and one relatively orthodox—may be describing the two main rival Jewish Christian sects, the Ebionites and the Nazarenes, respectively.[249]

Finally, the patristic descriptions of Jewish Christian sects provide some insight into the diversity and pervasiveness of Jewish Christianity in Palestine. In addition to the orthodox Nazarenes and the heretical sect (if not multiple sects) of the Ebionites, there were Gnostic Jewish Christians, such as Cerinthus. Symmachus, although possibly an Ebionite, may have emerged from descendants of the Pharisees. The Elkesaites, although not Jewish Christian themselves, appear to have been influenced by Jewish Christian ideas. Taken together, these groups demonstrate that Jewish Christianity was a diverse phenomenon with pervasive influence in Palestine in the first several centuries of the church's existence.

---

[248] Klijn and Reinink, *PE*, 71.
[249] Pritz, *Nazarene*, 21.

3

Theology of the Jewish Christians: Analysis of the Jewish Christian Gospels

There are numerous references in the patristic literature to the existence of Jewish Christian gospels written in the Hebrew language. There would seem to be no need to doubt that such gospels existed in some form, since Hebrew-speaking people would naturally wish to have a gospel in their own language. Unfortunately, none are extant today. All that remains are fragments contained in other, mainly patristic, sources. The oldest testimony we have to the existence of such a document comes from Papias via Eusebius. Papias (c. 60–130 CE) refers to a collection of the sayings of Jesus, made by Matthew in the Hebrew language, and he recalls a specific story about the woman accused of many sins.[250] Eusebius also reports that Hegesippus was aware of such a gospel.[251] Clement of Alexandria, writing in 202 or 215 CE, is the first writer to call this gospel the *Gospel According to the Hebrews*.[252] Following Clement in this is Origen.[253] Eusebius also mentions the gospel by name, but it is uncertain whether he actually saw it. Epiphanius mentions the name of the gospel once.[254] Didymus the Blind also mentions the gospel only once.[255] Jerome is the only Latin author to have claimed

---

[250] Eusebius, *hist. eccl.* 3.39.16–17 (*PE*, 143).

[251] Eusebius, *hist. eccl.* 4.22.8 (*PE*, 145).

[252] *Strom.*, 2.9.45.5 (*PE*, 111). It is unclear whether Clement personally viewed the gospel, although his references to it read as though he did.

[253] *in Joh.* 2.12 (*PE*, 127); *in Matth.* 15.14 (*PE*, 129).

[254] *pan.* 30.3.7 (*PE*, 179).

[255] Didymus, *in Psalmos* (*PE*, 199).

to have personally seen the gospel (in the Library of Caesarea), and he mentions it several times.[256]

Several conclusions may be drawn from this evidence. First, the fact that it is mentioned by Papias places the existence of a gospel in the Hebrew language as early as the late first century. Second, the fact that it was not cited by a specific name until the third century would seem to indicate that it was not named until relatively late.[257] Third, the specific name given, *Gospel According to the Hebrews*, would seem to indicate that its name was given by those patristic authors who referred to it, rather than by its author or by its direct Jewish Christian readers. Fourth, by the time the name *Gospel According to the Hebrews* appeared as a specific reference, the patristic authors appear to have lost direct contact with Jewish Christians. This can be seen in the fact that they lumped together all Jewish Christian groups under the term Ebionite. It can also be seen in the fact that the church fathers appeared to make no distinction between the versions of the gospel used by the various Jewish Christian groups, when in fact there were at least two: a *Gospel According to the Hebrews* used by the Nazarenes (henceforth referenced as the *Gospel of the Nazarenes*) and a *Gospel According to the Hebrews* used by the Ebionites (henceforth referenced as the *Gospel of the Ebionites*).[258] There may also have been a version of

---

[256] *de vir. ill.* 2 (*PE*, 20fl); *de vir. ill.* 3 (*PE*, 211); *in Mic.* 7.6 (*PE*, 209); *in Matth.* 12.13. (*PE*, 217).

[257] Up to the time that the Jewish and Gentile churches began to disassociate from each other, and especially after the church fathers began to label Jewish Christians as heretics generally, it seems likely that this Hebrew-language gospel would have been viewed simply as one of many existing versions of the Gospel According to Matthew. After that time there would have been a strong impetus to identify the gospel as belonging to a specific group. Of course, it is possible that some of the writers were simply unaware of the name, but this scenario seems unlikely for the reasons given in point four below.

[258] Pritz, *Nazarene*, 87; Vielhauer and Strecker, 135–136. Vielhauer and Strecker report that those with less confidence in Jerome suggest that there may have been at least three versions: the two listed above and a third which they simply call the Gospel of the Hebrews.

the *Gospel According to the Hebrews* used by the Jewish Christians in Egypt, though the evidence for this is less convincing.[259]

I. The Gospel of the Nazarenes

The text fragments of the *Gospel of the Nazarenes* demonstrate a close relationship with and a dependence upon the Gospel According to Matthew. It has been described as a "targum-like rendering of the canonical *Matthew*."[260] Therefore, its *terminus a quo* is the late first century (after the writing of Matthew) and its *terminus ad quem* is around 180 CE (when it was first mentioned by Hegesippus). Vielhauer and Strecker argue for a date of origin in the early first century. The fact that the Nazarene version of this gospel was originally written in Aramaic (Syriac) suggests that it may well have originated in or around Berea (Aleppo) in Coele-Syria, as indicated by Epiphanius and Jerome.[261]

There are several gospel fragments which have been attributed to the *Gospel of the Nazarenes*. However, for purposes of analyzing the theology and Christology of the Nazarene sect this analysis will be limited to those fragments (1) which are quoted by Jerome (since he was the only author to claim firsthand knowledge of the text), (2) which clearly apply to the Nazarenes, and (3) which provide some insight into the beliefs of the sect.

Applying these limitations to the available texts yields five fragments for consideration:

1. According to the Gospel written in Hebrew speech, which the Nazarenes read, "the whole fount of the Holy Spirit shall

---

[259] Pritz, *Nazarene*, 87; William Schneemelcher, "The Gospel of the Egyptians," *New Testament Apocrypha. Vol. I, Gospels and Related Writings*. ed. W. Schneemelcher (Philadelphia: Fortress, 1991), 214–215. Pritz believes that the Egyptians may have adapted their gospel from the Ebionite version. However, Schneemelcher reports that the *Gospel of the Egyptians* bears little resemblance to the canonical gospels and that some authorities believe that it was the gospel of the Gentile church in Egypt, although it does show some Jewish Christian influence.

[260] Vielhauer and Strecker, 159.

[261] Vielhauer and Strecker, 159.

descend upon him." Further in the Gospel which we have just mentioned, we find the following written:

And it shall come to pass when the Lord was come up out of the water, the whole fount of the Holy Spirit descended upon him and rested on him and said to him: "My Son, in all the prophets was I waiting for thee that thou shouldest come and I might rest in thee. For thou art my rest; thou art my first-begotten Son that reignest for ever."[262]

2. But in that Gospel written according to the Hebrews, which is read by the Nazoraeans [Nazarenes], the Lord says, "A moment ago my mother, the Holy Spirit, took me up." Nobody, however, should be scandalized because of this because the Spirit is used in the feminine gender with the Hebrews while our [Latin] language takes it in the masculine gender and in Greek the neuter.[263]

3. The Gospel called *According to the Hebrews* which was recently translated by me into Greek and Latin, which Origen frequently used, records after the resurrection of the Savior:

And when the Lord had given the linen cloth to the servant of the priest, he went to James and appeared to him. For James had sworn that he would not eat bread from that hour in which he had drunk from the cup of the Lord until he should see him risen from among them that sleep. And shortly thereafter the Lord said: "Take a table and bread!" And immediately it is added: he took bread, blessed it and brake it and gave it to James the Just and said to him: "My brother, eat thy bread, for the Son of Man is risen from among them that sleep."[264]

---

[262] Jerome, *in Esaiam* 11.2, quoted in Vielhauer and Strecker, 177; Pritz, *Nazarene,* 88; cf. Matt 3:16 cf. Heb 1:5ff; 5:5f; Isa 11:2; 61:1; Pss 132:14; Vielhauer and Strecker, 135–136. Vielhauer and Strecker note that those who suggest a third Gospel of the Hebrews place this text there.

[263] Jerome, *in Esaiam* 40.9–11 (*PE,* 225).

[264] Jerome, *de vir. ill.* 2, quoted in Vielhauer and Strecker, *Jewish-Christian Gospels,* 178; Pritz, *Nazarene,* 88; cf. 1 Cor 15:7; 11:23f; Vielhauer and Strecker, 135–136. Vielhauer and Strecker note that those who suggest a third Gospel of the Hebrews place this text there.

4. For since the apostles [sic] believed him to be a spirit according to the Gospel which is of the Hebrews and is read by the Nazarenes, a demon without a body, he said to them... [the rest of the text is missing].[265]

5. From the *Gospel According to the Hebrews*. In the *Gospel According to the Hebrews* which was written in the Chaldaic and Syriac language but with Hebrew letters, and is used up to the present day by the Nazoraeans [Nazarenes], I mean that according to the Apostles, or as many maintain, according to Matthew, which Gospel is also available in the Library of Caesarea, the story runs: sees the mother of the Lord and his brothers said to him: "John the Baptist baptizes for the remission of sins, let us go to be baptized by him." He [Jesus] said to them however: "What did I sin that I should go and be baptized by him? Unless perhaps that which I said in ignorance." And in the same volume: "If your brother," he said, "sinned to you with a word and makes amends, accept him seven times a day." Simon his disciple said to him: "Seven times a day?" The Lord answered and said to him: "And I say to you until seventy times seven. For even among the prophets after they were anointed with the Holy Spirit there were words of sin."[266]

In analyzing the first text, it seems clear the account of Jesus's baptism taken by Jerome from the *Gospel of the Nazarenes* is somewhat different from the one taken by Epiphanius from the *Gospel of the Ebionites* (see below).[267] The Nazarene baptism text has the Holy Spirit "descend" and "rest upon" Jesus, while the Ebionite baptism texts have the Holy Spirit "enter" Jesus. The Ebionite texts deny that Jesus was begotten of God the Father, while the Nazarene text supports a Christology of Jesus's sonship to God the Father consistent with that attributed to the Nazarenes in other

---

[265] Jerome *in Esaiam* 65 (*PE*, 227). Jerome compares this to Luke 24:38f.

[266] Jerome, *adv. Paleg.* 3.2 (*PE*, 227); cf. Matt 18:21f; Luke 17:4; Jas 3:2.

[267] Epiphanius, *pan.* 30.13.6–8 (*PE*, 179f).

places.[268] Because of Epiphanius's attestation that the Nazarenes accepted the virgin birth and the likelihood that the Nazarene gospel included a genealogy and the infancy narrative like that found in the canonical Gospel of Matthew, it seems unlikely that this text indicates an adoptionistic perspective. However, even if it did, this would not have been heretical by second-century standards. Interestingly, Pritz has suggested that the Nazarene Gospel's emphasis on sonship and the culmination of prophecy in the Messiah bears a strong resemblance to the Christology of the canonical *Epistle to the Hebrews*.[269] This similarity suggests at least a possible connection between the writer of that document and the community which produced the *Gospel of the Nazarenes*. It would certainly seem to indicate that the canonical *Epistle to the Hebrews* is of Jewish Christian origin.

From the second text, it should be noted that while the pneumatology represented is rather unsophisticated, it is no more primitive than that in evidence in the canonical gospels and is certainly not heretical. The reference to the Holy Spirit as Jesus's mother is intriguing (especially to modern, feminist theologians), but again is certainly not heretical, as even Jerome insists. This text is consistent with the account given elsewhere by Jerome. A similar account was given earlier in the writings of Origen, but Origen's account lacked Jerome's explanation of the Nazarene reference to the Holy Spirit as Christ's mother. This would appear to strengthen the assumption that Jerome had firsthand knowledge of the Hebrew-language text while Origen probably did not.[270] At the very least, the second text reflects the fact that Jerome's Hebrew was probably much better than Origen's, supporting Jerome's claim to have received extensive instruction in Hebrew from a Hebrew-speaking Jewish Christian.

---

[268] Epiphanius, *pan.* 29.7.3 (*PE*, 173); Jerome, *in Esaiam* 31.6–9 (*PE*, 223f).

[269] Pritz, *Nazarene,* 89; cf. Heb 1:5ff; 5:5f.

[270] Jerome variously describes the gospel as written in either Hebrew letters or Syriac (Aramaic). Given the reported location of the sect in Beroea, Aramaic seems the most likely possibility. This paper refers to this gospel as a "Hebrew-language" text to allow for both possibilities.

The third passage demonstrates a Nazarene belief in the resurrection of Christ, expanding on Epiphanius's earlier statement that the Nazarenes believed in the resurrection of the dead.[271] It is also worthy of note that the passage recounts that Jesus's first post-resurrection appearance was to James. While this appears out of sequence with the canonical gospels, a post-resurrection appearance to James is supported by Paul in his *First Letter to the Corinthians*[272] and is consistent with what is known from Epiphanius about the respect given to James by the Nazarenes.[273]

The fourth text, though attributed by Jerome to the Nazarenes, is argued by Pritz, Lightfoot, Vielhauer, and other authorities to have been attributed to the sect in error.[274] The Latin word *incorporale* (bodiless) comes from the Greek *asomaton* and therefore cannot have come from a Hebrew-language text.[275] Jerome may have taken it from Eusebius or Origen, who also quoted it but were unlikely to have been in contact with a Hebrew-language copy.[276] In fact, Origen actually attributes the text to a different document altogether: the *Doctrina Petri*.[277] In any case, this further underscores the likelihood that Jerome was dealing with a Hebrew-language version of the *Gospel of the Nazarenes* (albeit an incomplete one), while Eusebius and Origen were quoting from a Greek translation. Therefore, this text must be excluded from consideration as part of the *Gospel of the Nazarenes*.

The fifth text implies that the Nazarenes acknowledged the authority of the prophets. This sets the Nazarenes apart from the Ebionites, who rejected the authority of the prophets.[278] The fifth text makes note of Jesus's awareness of his own sinlessness as

---

[271] Pritz, *Nazarene,* 91; cf. *pan.* 29.7.3 (*PE,* 173).

[272] Pritz, *Nazarene,* 91; cf. 1 Cor 13:7.

[273] Pritz, *Nazarene,* 91; cf. *pan.* 29.4.3 (*PE,* 169).

[274] Pritz, *Nazarene,* 91f; cf. J. B. Lightfoot, *The Apostolic Fathers* (New York: Olms, 1973): 2.2.292; 296f.

[275] Pritz, *Nazarene,* 93.

[276] Eusebius, *hist. eccl.* 3.36.11 (*PE,* 143); Origen, *de princ.* 1 *praef.* 8 (*PE,* 125).

[277] *de princ.* 1 *praef.* 8 (*PE,* 125). This text is more closely associated with the Ebionites.

[278] Pritz, *Nazarene,* 93; cf. *pan.* 30.18.4–5 (*PE,* 187); *pan.* 29.7.2 (*PE,* 173).

compared to the prophets. One author even suggests that it may mean that they believed that Jesus had an awareness of his own divinity.[279] This is a very different Christology than the type of progressively increasing righteousness attributed to Jesus by the Ebionites.[280] While affirming Jesus's sinlessness, this text also affirms the possibility that he might be ignorant in some things. These paradoxical concepts find their counterparts in the canonical gospels of Luke and Mark[281] and would seem to indicate that the Nazarenes, like the rest of the early church, were wrestling with the concept of the dual nature of Christ.

II. The Gospel of the Ebionites

The fragments from the *Gospel of the Ebionites* suggest that it is synoptic in character, dependent on the gospels of Mark and Luke as well as Matthew. Therefore, its *terminus a quo* is the late first century (after the writing of the synoptic gospels), and its *terminus ad quem* is around 175 CE (when it was first mentioned by Irenaeus). Vielhauer and Strecker argue for a date of origin in the first half of the second century, probably later than the origin of the *Gospel of the Nazarenes.* It was originally written in Greek. Its place of origin is uncertain, but it is possible that it was written in the Transjordan area where the Ebionites made their home and where Epiphanius could have seen and copied from it.[282]

There are several gospel fragments which have been attributed to the *Gospel of the Ebionites.* However, for purposes of analyzing the theology and Christology of the Ebionite sect, this analysis will be limited to those fragments quoted by Epiphanius (who claims to have seen the text and copied from it) which provide some insight into the beliefs of the sect.

---

[279] J. T. Dodd, *The Gospel According to the Hebrews* (London: Search, 1933), 34, quoted in Pritz, *Nazarene*, 93.

[280] Hippolytus, *ref.* 7.34.1f (*PE*, 111f); Eusebius, *hist. eccl.* 3.27.2 (*PE*, 141); *pan.* 30.35ff (*PE*, 179).

[281] Pritz, *Nazarene*, 93; cf. Luke 2:52; Mark 12:32. Both texts demonstrate the limited nature of Jesus's knowledge.

[282] Vielhauer and Strecker, 169.

Applying these limitations to the available texts yields five fragments for consideration:

1. And the beginning of their Gospel runs:
    It came to pass in the days of Herod the king of Jude <when Caiaphas was high priest> that there came <one>, John <by name,> and baptized with the baptism of repentance in the river Jordan. It was said of him that he was of the lineage of Aaron the priest, a son of Zacharias and Elizabeth; and all went out to him.[283]

2. And after much has been recorded it proceeds:
    When the people were baptized Jesus also came and was baptized by John. And as he came up from the water, the heavens were opened and he saw the Holy Spirit in the form of a dove that descended and entered into him. And a voice sounded from heaven that said: "Thou art my beloved Son; in thee I am well pleased." And again: "I have this day begotten thee." And immediately a great light shone round about the place. When John saw this, it saith, he saith unto him: Who art thou, Lord? And again a voice from heaven (rang out) to him: "This is my beloved Son in whom I am well pleased." And then, it saith, John fell down before him and said: "I beseech thee, Lord, baptize thou me." But he prevented him and said: "Suffer it; for thus it is fitting that everything should be fulfilled."[284]

3. They say that he [Christ] was not begotten of God the Father, but created as one of the archangels...that he rules over the angels and all the creatures of the Almighty, and that he came

---

[283] Epiphanius, *pan.* 30.13.6, quoted in Vielhauer and Strecker, *Jewish-Christian Gospels*, 169; cf. Luke 1:5–18; 3:2f; Mark 1:4f; Matt 3:5. The text is likely a composite of two variant fragments of the same passage. The brackets would indicate where one of the texts contains words not found in the other.

[284] Epiphanius, *pan.* 30.13.7f, quoted in Vielhauer and Strecker, *Jewish-Christian Gospels,* 169; cf. Luke 3:21, 23; Matt 3:13, 16, 17, 14f; Mark 1:9, 11; Pss 2:7.

and declared, as their Gospel, which is called [*according to Matthew? according to the Hebrews?*], reports:

I am come to do away with sacrifices, and if ye cease not from sacrificing, the wrath of God will not cease from you.[285]

4. And it came to pass that John was baptizing; and there went out to him Pharisees and were baptized and all Jerusalem. And John had a garment of camel's hair and a leathern girdle about his loins, and his food, as it saith, was wild honey, he ate of which was that of manna, as a cake dipped in oil.

Thus, they were resolved to pervert the word of truth into a lie and put a cake in the place of locusts.[286]

5. But they abandon the proper sequence of the words and pervert the saying, as it is plain from all the readings attached and have let the disciples say:

Where wilt thou that we prepare the Passover? and him to answer to that: Do I desire with desire at this Passover to eat flesh with you?[287]

From the first text, it is notable that the Ebionites omit the nativity story (Matt 1–2) from their gospel. The Ebionites evidently denied the virgin birth. Jesus was considered God's Son not because he was divinely begotten, but because the Holy Spirit entered him at the time of his baptism by John, as mentioned in the second text. Taken together with the third text's emphasis on Jesus's not being begotten from the Father, the entry of the Holy Spirit described in the second text would seem to be different from the "descent" described in the canonical gospels,[288] probably denoting some form of adoptionism or Gnosticism. It is also somewhat different from the text in the

---

[285] Epiphanius, *pan.* 30.16.4f, quoted in Vielhauer and Strecker, *Jewish-Christian Gospels,* 170; cf. Matt 5:17f; John 3:36b.

[286] Epiphanius, *pan.* 30.13.41, quoted in Vielhauer and Strecker, *Jewish-Christian Gospels,* 169; cf. Matt 3:1, 7, 5, 4; Mark 1:14, 5, 6; Exod 16:31; Num 11:8.

[287] Epiphanius, *pan.* 30.22.4, quoted in Vielhauer and Strecker, *Jewish-Christian Gospels,* 170; cf. Matt 26:17ff. par.; Luke 22:15.

[288] Matt 3:16; Mark 1:10; Luke 3:22.

Gospel of the Nazarenes, which has the Holy Spirit "descend" and "rest upon" Jesus. The third text would seem to indicate that the Ebionites regarded Jesus as some sort of intermediate type of being, neither human nor divine.

The fourth text demonstrates the peculiar dietary rules of the sect. The omission of locusts from John's diet would support their vegetarian beliefs, though it should be noted that in Aramaic the term "locust" is a colloquialism for carob root. Their beliefs regarding the renunciation of meat are further supported by Jesus's rejecting of eating of flesh with his disciples on the Passover.

III. Summary and Conclusions

From the limited number of fragments available it is clear there was nothing in the extant fragments from the *Gospel of the Nazarenes* which was heretical in nature. These fragments show that the Nazarenes affirmed Jesus's resurrection from the dead. They appear to demonstrate a primitive, but not heretical, doctrine of the Holy Spirit; certainly not heretical in the second century, when the text was written. They seem to point to an understanding of the dual nature of Jesus, possibly including his own awareness of his divinity and humanity.

On the other hand, the extant fragments from the *Gospel of the Ebionites* demonstrate that their beliefs and Christology are distinct from those of the Nazarenes and clearly heretical. They demonstrate that the Ebionites rejected the virgin birth. They suggest an adoptionistic or Gnostic view of Jesus's divine sonship and relationship to the Holy Spirit. They imply a Christology in which Jesus is an intermediate creature, neither human nor divine. Finally, they illustrate the unique dietary rules of the sect.

Analyses of the fragmentary remains of the gospels produced by the Jewish Christians only serve to underscore the conclusions of the previous chapter. Of the five groups identified by the church fathers as Jewish Christians, only two met the definition of Jewish Christianity proposed by this study. These two groups were the Ebionites and the Nazarenes. Analysis of the *Gospel of the Ebionites* confirms that their Christology was heretical, as the church fathers testified. However, as far as can be discerned from the fragments of the *Gospel of the Nazarenes*, there was nothing about their theology which lay outside the bounds of orthodoxy at the time the gospel was originally written.

4

Corroborating the Church Fathers: Analysis of Archaeological, Talmudic, and Other Sources

A significant problem in the study of Jewish Christianity is how much reliability to ascribe to the major source of information on specific Jewish Christian groups: the testimony of the church fathers. What we have in the patristic data is information on Jewish Christian groups which has been preserved by their adversaries: those who proclaimed the groups to be heretical. At the very least this raises the possibility that the patristic authors might slant the data to support their own pre-existing opinions. Therefore, corroborative data from other sources is desirable. This chapter will attempt to corroborate the information provided by the church fathers using data from non-patristic sources. These sources include archaeological data, Jewish Talmudic sources, and other historical sources.

I. Archaeological Data

The nature of the available archaeological data related to Jewish Christianity, although appearing to be relatively plentiful, cannot be used to shed light on the theology or practices of any specific Jewish Christian group. For example, most of the archaeological evidence is found in the graffiti on ossuaries and on the walls of tombs, grottos, and ruins. The evidence consists mostly of symbols, names, and other information that strongly suggest that some member of a Jewish Christian group inhabited the site, but which do not permit identification of the specific group. However, the archaeological evidence can provide some important corroborative information.

The archaeological data is also useful in establishing the geographic and historical extent of Jewish Christianity.

Bagatti, Mancini, and others argue that evidence of Jewish Christianity has been noted at more than forty sites throughout the area which constituted ancient Palestine. These sites included Jerusalem, Bethany, Bethphage, Bethlehem, Talpiot (between Jerusalem and Bethlehem), Amwas (a possible Emmaus road site), Tiberias, Caesarea, and Wadi Muraba'at in Judea; Nazareth, Kaukab (near Nazareth), K'far Nahum (Capernaum), Sephoris, Bainah, K'far Semai and Saknin[289] (near Sephoris), Beth ha-Shitta (near Beth Shean), and Khirbet Kilkish in Galilee and Samaria; Pella; Allepo (ancient Berea) and other sites in Syria; and elsewhere.[290] The limitations of this study do not permit a comprehensive analysis of the available archaeological data. However, a review of the data from several selected sites can add useful corroborative data to that available from the patristic sources.

A. Jerusalem

In Jerusalem, at the Church of the Resurrection (a.k.a. Church of the Holy Sepulcher) excavators in 1971 broke through a wall under the eastern end of the building and discovered a small room containing a pre-Constantinian (perhaps as early as the first half of the second century CE) red and black drawing of a small sailing vessel with the inscription *"DOMINE IVIMUS"* (Latin for "Lord, we went"). Some have speculated that this represents the return to Jerusalem of the Jewish Christian congregation which fled during the fall of Jerusalem. Others speculate that it represents an early Gentile Christian pilgrimage.[291]

---

[289] Cf. Bagatti, 95ff. Saknin may recall the name of K'far Sechania, birthplace of the *min Jacob* referred to in some Talmudic texts.

[290] J. Danielou, "Review of Archaeological Discoveries Relative to the Jewish-Christians by Ignacio Mancini." In *Recherches de Science Religieuse* 58 (1970): 143–145.143–145; Bagatti, 4; Saunders, 204; cf. Mancini. Evidence has also been found in Jordan, Sinai, and as far away as Rome.

[291] E. M. Meyers, "Early Judaism and Christianity in the Light of Archaeology," *Biblical Archaeology*, 51(2) (1988): 77.

At Bat'n el-Hawa (Mount of Scandal) in Jerusalem, a local Arab found thirty ossuaries dating from the first and second centuries CE in a room carved from the rook. Archaeologist C. Clermont Ganneau, who studied the ossuaries, concluded that they covered several generations, that they belonged to one family, and that some of the members whose remains were buried there were Jewish Christians. He gave several reasons for his conclusion: (1) some of the ossuaries were marked with Christian-sounding proper names (e.g., Kyrikos); (2) some of the ossuaries were marked with a variety of Christian symbols (e.g., an "X" before the name "Jesus" spelled in Greek); and (3) one ossuary was marked with a finely-chiseled cross under the name "Jude."[292] Eleazar Sukenik, professor of archaeology at Hebrew University, discovered similar evidence at Talpiot, on the Jerusalem-Bethlehem road. Among the ossuaries there, he found two which were inscribed in Greek with the name "Jesus," followed by the words *iou* (the beginning of the word *Ioudah* or "Jude") and *alot* (an exclamation of grief).[293] Similarly, at the so-called *Tombs of Sanhedra* the Israeli scholar Julius Jotham-Rothschild discovered, among a series of *kokhim* (i.e., small, oven-shaped graves carved into rock), three *kokhim* which were marked with crosses.[294] These sites demonstrate the early presence of Jewish Christians in Jerusalem, as well as a continuing contact between Jews and Jewish Christians. They also support Schiffman's claim that Jewish Christians, though considered heretical by their fellow Jews, were not considered non-Jews and were not denied their basic right to rest among their ancestors.[295]

---

[292] C. Clermont-Ganneau, *Archaeological Researches in Palestine During the Years* (1989), 381–412; in Mancini, *Archaeology,* 14–15.

[293] Eleazar L. Sukenik, "The Earliest Records of Christianity," *American Journal of Archaeology* 51(1947): 351–365; in Mancini, *Archaeology,* 19–20.

[294] Julius Jotham-Rothschild, "The Tombs of Sanhedra," *Palestine Exploration Quarterly* 84 (1952): 23–38; 86 (1954): 16–22; in Mancini, *Archaeology,* 27–28.

[295] Schiffman, 6ff; cf. Mancini, 28.

B. The Judean Desert

At Muraba'at, J. T. Milik discovered a letter by Simeon Bar Kokhba which apparently threatened Galilean Jewish-Christians with imprisonment if they did not aid in his rebellion. If Milik was correct in his interpretation that the intended recipients of the letter were in fact Jewish Christians, then this letter provides important information about their situation during the Second Jewish Revolt. Evidently, they took a non-combatant stance, which could have been based either on Jesus's teachings or in reaction to R. Akiva's proclamation of Bar Kokhba as Messiah. The letter also suggests that this stance led to further enmity between Jews and Jewish Christians.[296]

C. Galilee

In Capernaum on the northwest shore of the Sea of Galilee, next to the octagonal Byzantine Church of St. Peter at Capernaum, lie the remains of a Jewish Christian house church which dates to the first century CE. The church has been expanded several times from the original structure, which local tradition holds was Peter's house. Next to these ruins are the remains of a series of Jewish synagogues dating from the first to the fifth centuries. Also nearby are the ruins of Gentile Christian sites. By following the strata and the structures researchers have determined that Jewish Christians occupied the site from the first through the seventh centuries CE. This site is also important in that it demonstrates a prolonged period of contact between Jews and Jewish Christians as well as between Jewish and Gentile Christians.[297] In Nazareth, at the Basilica of the Annunciation to Mary, excavations have discovered Jewish Christian graffiti dating prior to the Council of Ephesus (431 CE), and other graffiti and monuments which they believe establish beyond doubt that the shrine was occupied by Jewish Christians through the end of the fifth century.[298] In nearby Beth ha-Shitta,

---

[296] J. T. Milik, "Une lettre de Semeon Bar Kokeba," *Revue Biblique* 60 (1953): 276–294; in Mancini, *Archaeology,* 38–40.

[297] Meyers, 76–77; cf. Mancini, 100–103; 177.

[298] Mancini, 68ff.

Aharoni and Avi-Yonah found a building with a mosaic floor, the letters and symbols of which established it to be of Jewish Christian origin. They estimate that the mosaic dates to 614 CE, establishing a Jewish Christian presence in the area through the end of the seventh century.[299]

D. Syria and Transjordan

In Tafas, in Syria, researchers found the remains of a building which included several inscriptions including the following: "James and Samuel and Clematios, their father, built this synagogue." Taking into account the place of discovery and other inscriptions (e.g., crosses, sacred letters, references to angels, and various symbols), the researchers concluded that this had been a Jewish Christian synagogue.[300] Similar inscriptions, mostly of a funerary nature, have been found in the Kerak district of Transjordan.[301] Because Tafas is very near the site of ancient Kochaba and not far from Pella, which lies in the Kerak district, these sites corroborate several aspects of Epiphanius's testimony regarding the Nazarenes and the Ebionites. These sites tend to support his claims that the Nazarenes settled in the area of Pella after the fall of Jerusalem, that the Ebionites split off from them and moved on to settle at Kochaba, and that the Ebionites worshiped in synagogues rather than churches.[302]

E. Conclusions

The archaeological data tends to provide some support for the assertions of the church fathers regarding Jewish Christianity. Specifically, it lends some support to the tradition of the Jewish

---

[299] Y. Aharoni, "Excavations at Beth-Hashitta," *Bulletin of the Israeli Exploration Society* 18 (1954), 209–215; in Mancini, *Archaeology,* 83–85.

[300] J. B. Frey, *Corpus Inscription Judicarium* 861; in Mancini, *Archaeology,* 44.

[301] Reginetta Canova, *Iscrizioni e monumenti procristiani nel paese di Moab* (Citta del Vaticano, (1954); in Mancini, *Archaeology,* 45.

[302] Epiphanius, *pan.* 29.7.8 (*PE*, 173); 30.2.8 (*PE*, 175); cf. Eusebius, *hist. eccl.* 3.5.3 (*PE*, 139).

Christian flight to Pella and claims that Pella and Kochaba were centers, respectively, for Nazarene and Ebionite activity.

On the other hand, the archaeological data tends to demonstrate that Jewish Christianity may have been far more prevalent over a longer period than would seem to be indicated by the patristic literature.[303] While some of the data is controversial,[304] if Bagatti's and Mancini's interpretations of the archaeological evidence are accepted, clearly the practice of Jewish Christianity was at one time quite extensive not only in Palestine but in the surrounding areas. In addition, archaeological evidence tends to rebut the argument that Jewish Christianity died out quickly after either 70 CE or 135 CE. According to Mancini and others, there is evidence of active Jewish Christianity, especially in the hill country of Palestine, through the fourth century, followed by a state of decline for another century or two.[305] It is clear that at one time Jewish Christianity was the dominant expression of the Christian Church in Palestine. The archaeological data opens the question of how long it remained so. Some have suggested that it was the dominant church in the area until the time of Constantine and the arrival of Byzantine Christians. Since many of the Jewish Christian sites stand in close proximity to Gentile Christian sites, the archaeological evidence appears to document a struggle for dominance between the native Jewish Christian community and the incoming Gentile Christian authorities, with Gentile and Jewish Christian churches existing side by side in the same towns dating from the fourth century.[306] It is the opinion of Mancini and others that it was not until the arrival of the Byzantines that Jewish

---

[303] Although the patristic authors do not state this explicitly, from reading the patristic information on Jewish Christianity, one gets the impression that by the middle of the second century Jewish Christianity was limited to a few fringe groups and that it died out by the end of the fourth century.

[304] Saunders, 204. Saunders faults Mancini for the sometimes-uncritical way in which he reports the data. The data at some of the sites is open to varying interpretations as to whether it was left by Jewish Christians, "Judaizing" Gentile Christians, or non-native Jews. However, the preponderance of evidence in most cases points to Jewish Christianity.

[305] Mancini, 176–177.

[306] Mancini, 177.

Christians were finally outnumbered, divided, and marginalized, and began to slip away into heretical sects.[307]

II. Talmudic References

Little attention has been given to Jewish sources in the study of Jewish Christianity. The Talmudic references to Jewish Christianity are limited but do provide helpful background data. First, the data from Jewish sources would tend to support Epiphanius's claim that the earliest Jewish Christians in Palestine were called Nazarenes. There are at least a dozen Talmudic texts which use the term Nazarene(s) to describe either Jesus (*Yeshu ha-Nozri*) and/or his followers (*ha-Nozrim*).[308] Researchers agree that the events referred to by the earliest text occurred no later than 130 CE. However, some evidence exists which could place these events in this text as early as 90 CE.[309] The text describes a person named Jacob from the town of K'far Sechania in Galilee who was a follower of Jesus the Nazarene and who engaged synagogue Jews in discussions about Jesus.[310] It is reasonable to assume from his name and locality that he was a Jew. It is also reasonable to assume that, since the text states that Jacob was an old man at the time of these incidents, he may well have been born prior to 70 CE. Therefore, it would not be unreasonable to assume that the name Nazarene was the name used prior 70 CE by Jews to describe Jewish Christians. (By the middle of the third century, Jews appear to have begun using the term to describe Christians generally, an understandable transfer as

---

[307] Saunders, 204; cf. Bagatti; Mancini.

[308] *Sanh.* 107b, (twice); 43a (four times); *Sota* 47a; *av. Zar.* 16b–17a (twice); *Taanit* 27b; quoted in Pritz, *Nazarene,* 95. Pritz does not provide the full citations.

[309] Pritz, *Nazarene*, 96f; Schiffman, *Who Was a Jew?*, 70; cf. *Av. Zar.* 16b–17a, quoted in Pritz, *Nazarene*, 96; *tHul* 2:22–23, quoted in Schiffman, *Who Was a Jew?,* 69f. The dating is based on the appearance of R. Eliezer b. Hyrkanos in the text. However, Pritz argues that the text is evocative of Roman persecution of Christians and may therefore be placed around 109 CE.

[310] *Av. Zar.* 16b–17a, quoted in Pritz, *Nazarene*, 96; *tHul* 2:22–23, quoted in Schiffman, *Who Was a Jew?,* 69f. See earlier notes for information on the dating of this text.

Christianity became increasingly Gentile.[311]) Similarly, since this text also shows a Nazarene presence in Galilee at the beginning of the second century, it demonstrates a continuity of Nazarene Jewish Christianity after the destruction of the temple in 70 CE.[312] Another early passage describes the cursing of K'far Sechania because it did not mourn for Jerusalem.[313] This is likely a memory of the split which occurred between Jews and Jewish Christians at the time of the destruction of Jerusalem.[314] The Pharisees went west and at Yavne began a consolidation of Judaism which eventually became rabbinical Judaism. After the crisis of 70 CE, the diversity of first-century Judaism—which had included Pharisees, Sadducees, Essenes, Zealots, and no doubt others, as well as Nazarene Jewish Christians—was no longer deemed acceptable. The Nazarenes, and likely others, were quickly excluded. The Nazarenes went east and, rejecting the consolidation begun at Yavne, engaged in evangelism among their Jewish brothers and sisters in the synagogues.[315]

Along similar lines, there is evidence that the *Birkat ha-Minim* (a curse against apostates in the twelfth benediction of the *Shemoneh-Esreh* prayer in the daily *Amidah*) arose in response to the evangelistic activities of Nazarene Jewish Christians such as the *min* Jacob of K'far Sechania. Most scholars now believe that the *Birkat ha-Minim* was composed sometime between 80 CE and 95 CE.[316] Examination of fragments of the *Shemoneh-Esreh* prayer

---

[311] *B. Taanit* 27b; cf. Pritz, *Nazarene*, 98–99.

[312] cf. *B. Gittin* 57a, quoted in Pritz, *Nazarene*, 99–100.

[313] *B. Gittin* 57, quoted in Pritz, *Nazarene*, 99–100. The village was considered to have become spiritually *meshamud* (Heb. for apostate/traitorous).

[314] Pritz, *Nazarene,* 101. Perhaps the Nazarene Jews, considering Jesus's prophecy regarding the destruction of the temple, would not have taken its destruction quite as hard as their non-Nazarene brothers and sisters. Perhaps they even used Jesus's prediction of the destruction of the temple as evangelistic evidence. Certainly later Gentiles saw it this way: not only as a confirmation of Jesus's prophecy but as punishment of the Jews for the crucifixion of Jesus.

[315] Pritz, *Nazarene*, 101.

[316] *B. Brach* 28b, quoted in Pritz, *Nazarene,* 104. *B. Brach* 25b records the following: "Said R. Gamaliel to the Sages: 'Can anyone among you frame a benediction relating to the *minim*?' Samuel the Lesser arose and composed it." Pritz notes that the elevation of Gamaliel to *nasi* and the death

found at the Cairo Geniza excavation in Egypt has demonstrated that the earliest versions of the twelfth benediction included the words: "may the *nozrim* [Nazarenes] and the *minim* [sectarians] perish in a moment."[317] Based on this and other information, Pritz, Schiffman, and others argue that the *Birkat ha-Minim* was originally developed in response to the Nazarene Jewish Christians.[318] Along similar lines, it is instructive to note that the term *minim,* although in use before the origin of Jewish Christianity, had always referred to Jews who see themselves as Jews, but who were excluded by the rabbis.[319] They were not considered non-Jews, but rather apostate Jews, in the hope that they might someday return to the truth and be readmitted to the community.[320]

The Talmudic sources provide corroboration for several patristic claims. They tend to reinforce Epiphanius's claim that the term Nazarene was used to describe Jewish Christians generally in the first century. They also generally support his arguments about the location of the Nazarene sect as well as Jerome's contention that the Nazarenes were in continued contact with and actively involved in evangelism among their Jewish brothers and sisters in the synagogues. Finally, they support patristic claims that the Nazarenes were cursed in the synagogues by their Jewish brethren.

---

of Shmuel *ha-qatan* are known to have occurred between the above dates, leading most scholars to agree on the date of this passage.

[317] Solomon Schechter, "Geniza Specimens," *Jewish Quarterly Review* 10 (1897/8): 654–659; J. Mann, "Geniza Fragments of the Palestinian Order of Service," *Hebrew Union College Annual* 2 (1925), 306; cf. Pritz, *Nazarene,* 104; Meyers, 70.

[318] Pritz, *Nazarene,* 104; Schiffman, 61.

[319]Louis Finkelstein, "The Development of the Amidah." *Jewish Quarterly Review* 16 (1925–1926): 156.

[320] Schiffman, 61. Schiffman notes: "It cannot be overemphasized that while the benediction against the *minim* sought to exclude Jewish Christians from active participation in the synagogue service, it in no way implied expulsion from the Jewish people. In fact, heresy, no matter how great, was ever seen as cutting the heretic's tie to Judaism. Not even outright apostasy could never overpower the balakhic criteria for Jewish identification. Indeed, regardless of the transgressions of a Jew, he was a Jew under any and all circumstances, even though his rights within *halakah* might be limited because of his actions." The classification of Jewish Christians as non-Jews is a relatively modem phenomenon.

III. The Pella Tradition

The church fathers Eusebius and Epiphanius both describe what has come to be called the Pella tradition. Eusebius mentions it once. Epiphanius mentions it three times in two different documents.[321] The core of the Pella tradition has three parts: (1) the miraculous escape of the Jewish Christian community from Jerusalem; (2) their relocation to Pella in the Transjordan; and (3) the subsequent fall of Jerusalem.[322] Epiphanius adds their eventual return to Jerusalem prior to 129 CE.

Recently, some authorities have challenged the authenticity of the Pella tradition. Lüdemann offers several arguments against the tradition primarily based on literary criticism. First, he suggests that the sources of the tradition have a relatively late date of origin, dating back only to the second century. Second, he asserts that the sources for the tradition all originate from the vicinity of Pella. Third, he argues that there are few sources, limited to the writings of the church fathers, and some of them depend upon others (e.g., he argues that Epiphanius depends on Eusebius). Fourth, he contends that the tradition conflicts with assertions of second-century sources that a Jewish Christian congregation continued in Jerusalem after 70 CE. Therefore, Lüdemann argues, the tradition probably was fabricated in the second century by the Jewish Christian community in Pella to legitimize themselves based on apostolic authority.[323]

Brandon takes a more historical approach in his argument against the Pella tradition. First, he argues that one would have expected that if the Jerusalem congregation had survived and some had returned to Jerusalem, the Jerusalem church would not have lost the preeminent authority which it held prior to 70 CE. Second, he contends that Pella would not have been a safe haven for Jewish Christians, since Jewish Zealots had razed the town in 66 CE, likely

---

[321] Eusebius, *hist. eccl.* 3.5.3 (*PE*, 139); Epiphanius, *pan.* 29.7.7–8 (*PE*, 173); 30.2.7 (*PE*, 177); *Weights* 15, quoted in Craig Koester, "The Origin and Significance of the Flight to Pella Tradition," *The Catholic Bible Quarterly* 51(1989): 93.

[322] Koester, 91.

[323] Lüdemann, 200–210; cf. Koester, 105.

arousing the inhabitants' animosity toward Jews of any stripe.[324] Third, he suggests that it would have been extremely difficult to leave Jerusalem, which was being guarded by Zealots on the inside and surrounded by Roman siege lines on the outside.[325]

The case for the historicity and orthodoxy of the Nazarenes does not directly depend on the historicity of the Pella tradition. However, since most of the explicit information concerning the Nazarenes comes from Epiphanius, any data which corroborates Epiphanius's claims about the Nazarenes is helpful in establishing his credibility.

Koester has responded convincingly to Lüdemann's argument, using several independent sources to establish the historicity of the Pella tradition.[326] First, there appears to be at least one first-century source which supports the tradition, the New Testament evidence being stronger than Lüdemann allows. The Gospel According to Luke (21:20–22) appears to make implicit reference to all three elements of the tradition:

20 When you see Jerusalem surrounded by armies, then know that its desolation has come near.

21 Then those in Judea must flee to the mountains and those inside the city must leave it, and those out in the country must not enter it,

22 for those are days of vengeance as a fulfillment of all that is written.

If this assumption is true, then Luke's comment in verse 20 about Jerusalem being "surrounded by armies" would refer to the fall of Jerusalem. Verse 21 would refer to the escape of Jerusalem's Jewish Christian community. Verse 21 would also refer to the relocation of the community to safety in the mountains. While Luke did not make explicit reference to Pella as the relocation site, it is worth noting that Pella is located in the foothills of the Transjordan highlands,

---

[324] Josephus, *War.* 2.457–460.

[325] Raymond Pritz, "On Brandon's Rejection of the Pella Tradition," *Immanuel* 13 (1981): 39–43.

[326] Koester, 90–106.

consistent with Luke's account.[327] While this does not prove that the tradition was known in the first century, it does at least suggest it, making a first-century date possible.

Second, Koester contends that in addition to Luke's account, there are independent attestations of the tradition from several sources, not all from the Pella region. The Syriac version of the Pseudo-Clementine *Recognitions,* dating from the mid-second century, also provides a strong implicit reference to the tradition. This document referred to: (1) a war which would occur after the "coming of the true prophet," during which unbelievers would be destroyed and expelled from their places of sacrifice;[328] (2) the redemption (and return) of those who "kept the law without sacrifices";[329] and (3) their relocation to a "secure place of the land" so "that they might survive and be preserved."[330] Koester argues that the references to war and destruction correspond to the Pella tradition's references to the fall of Jerusalem. The redemption of those who "kept the law without sacrifice" parallels the tradition's flight of the Jewish Christian community from the city. Finally, he suggests that the "secure place of land" was an implicit reference to the relocation to Pella.[331] Koester argues that Eusebius learned of the tradition from a source other than the Pseudo-Clementine *Recognitions* since Eusebius made explicit reference to Pella, while the *Recognitions* did not. Koester suggests that Eusebius's source was probably Ariston of Pella. Epiphanius's discussion of the tradition, Koester contends, can be demonstrated to be independent of both *Recognitions* and Eusebius. Textual analyses of the passages show few similarities and significant differences, and Epiphanius's description lacks the theological shaping of either the *Recognitions* or the Eusebius account. Therefore, one cannot assume that Epiphanius drew from a Pella source for his discussion of the Pella tradition.[332]

---

[327] Koester, 103f.

[328] *Recog.* 137.19–47; cf. 2.39.31–42; quoted in Koester, *Origin and Significance,* 98–99.

[329] *Recog.* 1.37.36–37; quoted in Koester, *Origin and Significance,* 99.

[330] *Recog.* 1.37.14–15; quoted in Koester, *Origin and Significance,* 98.

[331] Koester, 101–103.

[332] Koester, 105.

Third, there are a number of reasonable explanations why the Pella tradition is not clearly attested in early Christian writings. None of the extant texts suggests that any of the apostles went to Pella. This would have removed any special status from those who went and returned from Pella, since early Christian writers were more concerned with tracking the movements of apostles than those of individual congregations.[333] Also, the Nazarenes' observance of the ceremonial law (not to mention the heretical theology of the Ebionites) increasingly isolated them from the greater church.[334] The story of the founding of a congregation which the greater church increasingly viewed as heretical would not have been a matter of general interest to Christians.[335]

Finally, the traditions of a continuing Christian presence in Jerusalem after 70 CE do not necessarily conflict with the Pella tradition. The tradition's claim that the entire community left may be an overstatement, or perhaps a large number from the community returned relatively quickly after the fall of Jerusalem. Based on these arguments, Koester concludes that the most likely explanation of the Pella tradition is that it is the memory of actual first-century events.

Responding to Brandon's objections, Pritz offers the following arguments in support of the Pella tradition. First, Brandon's argument against the tradition rests in part on the assumption that the survival of the Jerusalem congregation would have ensured its continued preeminent position of authority in the greater church. However, Brandon overlooks the fact that in the primitive church authority rested not on place but on relationship to Jesus. For example, James was not the final authority because he was the bishop of Jerusalem; rather he was chosen bishop of Jerusalem because of the authority he held by virtue of the fact that he was the brother of Jesus. Brandon's argument for place-oriented authority looks for an anachronism—a concept of "apostolic

---

[333] Koester, 105.

[334] cf. *pan.* 29.7.5–7; *Recog.* 143.2; quoted in Koester, *Origin and Significance*, 106.

[335] Koester, 106.

succession"—that did not become a working reality until at least a century later.[336]

Second, Brandon's argument against the Pella tradition rests on the assumption that the town would not have been a safe refuge for any Jews, even Jewish Christians, since it had been sacked— along with several other Syrian towns—by Jewish Zealots during the war. However, Josephus's *Jewish Wars* provides evidence which refutes this assumption and provides support for the notion of Pella as a city of refuge for Jewish Christians. Josephus noted that the local Jewish populations of several of the cities stood alongside their Gentile neighbors, attempting to repel the attacking Zealots.[337] He also recorded that the inhabitants of one of the cities had protected and supported their Jewish neighbors.[338] So it is by no means certain that the Jewish Christian refugees from Jerusalem would have been denied refuge by the inhabitants of Pella. Furthermore, Pritz suggests that it was likely that Pella contained a large community of Greek Christians, who would have been much more likely to have provided refuge for the Jewish Christian refugees than would a community composed entirely of non-Christian Gentiles.[339]

Finally, Brandon's argument against the Pella tradition rests on the assumption that it would have been impossible for the Jerusalem congregation to escape the city while it was under siege. On the contrary, Josephus provides confirmation of several such large escapes taking place right up until the end of the siege. Many of the leaders of the city escaped in 66 CE.[340] Four separate escapes occurred during the winter of 67–68 CE (before Pesach),[341] one of

---

[336] Pritz, "Pella," 40–41. Also, as noted above, early Christian writers were more concerned with tracking the movements of apostles than those of individual congregations.

[337] Pritz, "Pella," 41–42; cf. *War.* 2:466–468; quoted in Flavius Josephus, *The Works of Josephus,* translated by William Wiston (Peabody, MA: Hendrickson, 1987): 627.

[338] Pritz, "Pella," 41–42; cf. *War.* 2.450; quoted in Josephus, 628.

[339] Pritz, "Pella," 42.

[340] Pritz, "Pella," 43; cf. *War.* 2.538, quoted in Josephus, 631; 2.556, quoted in Josephus, 633.

[341] Pritz, "Pella," 43; cf. *War.* 4.353, quoted in Josephus, 681; 4.377ff, quoted in Josephus, 682; 4.397, quoted in Josephus, 683; 4.410, quoted in Josephus, 681.

which included 2,000 people.[342] Another four escapes occurred in 70 CE,[343] one of which included the chief priests and the aristocracy.[344] Not until the temple was burned did Titus forbid further desertions,[345] yet even after this decree 40,000 inhabitants of Jerusalem turned themselves in to the Romans and were allowed to go free.[346] On the basis of the above arguments and the evidence from Josephus, Pritz argues that first-century Jewish Christians did, in fact, escape Jerusalem and flee to Pella.

A. Conclusions

Although the Pella tradition has been the subject of some criticism of late, its historicity appears to be strengthened by data from several sources. These sources include the Gospel According to Luke, the Pseudo-Clementine *Recognitions*, Josephus's *Jewish Wars*, and the likely non-patristic sources of Eusebius and Epiphanius.

IV. Summary and Conclusions

This chapter has succeeded in corroborating the church fathers on several points. The archaeological data tends to support the patristic evidence that the Nazarenes and the Ebionites existed through the fourth century. The testimony of the church fathers regarding the location of the Nazarenes and Ebionites in the area around Pella and Kochaba receives support from the archaeological data, the Talmudic data, and the Pseudo-Clementine *Recognitions*. Similarly, the tradition of the flight of the Jewish Christian community from Jerusalem to Pella receives support from the archaeological data, the Pseudo-Clementine *Recognitions*, and from Josephus's *Jewish Wars*. The Talmudic sources also provide corroboration for several other claims, including Epiphanius's contention that the term

---

[342] Pritz, "Pella," 43; cf. *War.* 4.353, quoted in Josephus, 681.

[343] Pritz, "Pella," 43; cf. *War.* 5.4201ff, quoted in Josephus, 718f; 5.446–450, quoted in Josephus, 720; 5.551ff, quoted in Josephus, 720; 6.113–115, quoted in Josephus, 732f.

[344] Pritz, "Pella," 43; cf. *War.* 6.113–115, quoted in Josephus, 732f.

[345] Pritz, "Pella," 43; cf. *War.* 6.352, quoted in Josephus, 745.

[346] Pritz, "Pella," 43; cf. *War.* 6.383–386, quoted in Josephus, 747.

"Nazarene" was used to describe Jewish Christians generally in the first century; Jerome's assertion that the Nazarenes were in continued contact with and actively involved in evangelism among synagogue Jews; and claims that the Nazarenes were cursed in the synagogues. All these factors tend to lend credibility to the testimonies of the church fathers, particularly Epiphanius and Jerome, about the Nazarenes.

On the other hand, the archaeological data suggests that Jewish Christianity was far more prevalent over a longer period than the church fathers seem to allow. Despite the controversial nature of some of the archaeological data, it is clear that Jewish Christianity was at one time the dominant expression of the Christian Church in Palestine, remaining so until perhaps the time of Constantine and the arrival of Byzantine Christians. The archaeological data suggests that Jewish Christianity was active through the fourth century, then fell into period of decline, but may have hung onto existence for at least another century before fading out of existence. Therefore, while the archaeological data tends to dispute the church fathers on this point, it does support the thesis that Jewish Christian groups were in existence through at least the fourth century.

5

From Acceptance Through Ambivalence to Antipathy: The Changing Attitude of the Church Fathers toward Jewish Christianity

It is clear that the church's attitude towards Jewish Christianity changed significantly over the first four centuries. The attitudes of the first century apostles were generally tolerant of Jewish Christianity, taking it to be acceptable, if not normative. The second century was a time of transformation in which Jewish Christianity rapidly became the exception rather than the rule, considered a valid, if archaic, expression of Christianity. However, by the time of the third and fourth centuries, the church fathers appear to view any expression of Jewish Christianity, regardless of the theology behind it, as heretical. This change in attitude represented a massive reversal of opinion. It evolved over several centuries, shaped by a variety of complex and interconnected forces. This chapter will attempt to describe both the outward content of the change and the forces that shaped it. In view of the paucity of sources, such a general history of the changing attitude of the church fathers toward Jewish Christianity can only be sketchy and provisional at best. Nonetheless, even such a provisional history may clarify how the church could have moved from an exclusively Jewish Christian institution to an institution that excluded Jewish Christians.

I. Setting the Stage:
A Roman Holocaust in the Holy Land

The separation of rapidly expanding Gentile Christian movement from what would become synagogue Judaism, and the virtual excommunication of the Jewish Christian movement by both, cannot be completely understood without comprehending the impact or the nature of Roman occupation of Palestine (or as they thought of it, Roman Palestine).

Even by Roman Imperial standards, the occupation of Roman Palestine was exceptionally brutal, amounting to what today we would call genocide. Historians estimate that between 100 BCE and 100 CE fully one-third of the population of the region was executed by the occupying Roman legions. Crucifixion was a daily occurrence. It was reported that the roads entering cities of any significant size were regularly lined with dozens of crosses, still bearing the bodies of the crucified. Technically speaking, crucifixion was legally reserved solely for the worst enemies of Rome: those convicted of treason. Practically speaking, however, Roman authorities defined the crime of treason loosely: any action against the interests of the Empire could suffice. When "examples" were needed—victims to serve as an example of what happened if one stood against the Empire—sufficient grounds could be found.

What does this kind of brutal oppression do to a people? It ultimately splinters them, exacerbating tensions, widening existing divisions, and creating new ones. The Romans may not have used the term "Stockholm Syndrome," but they were certainly aware of the peculiar dynamics of oppressed peoples. Studies of the effects of oppression on the social behavior of oppressed peoples have noted a counterintuitive phenomenon. Given the fact that the Roman legions were a distinct minority wherever they ruled, logic would dictate that if all the oppressed people of a particular region joined forces, they might have a fighting chance of throwing off their oppressors. Instead, they turned on each other in order to divert their oppressors' attention from themselves to someone else.

It is this broader conflict—this genocidal occupation, and its peculiar conditioning of the peoples of the area—that forms the backdrop for the more focused conflict among the emerging Judaisms, Christianities, and Jewish Christianities beginning early in the first century.[348]

---

[348] Daniel Boyarin explores this context from a Jewish perspective in two books: *Borderlines: The Partition of Judeao-Christianity.* Philadelphia, PA: University of Pennsylvania Press, 2006; and *A Radical Jew: Paul and the Politics of Identity.* Berkley, CA: University of California Press, 1994. From Boyarin's

II. In the Beginning:
A Jewish Christian Church

It is clear that, at its beginning, the church was a Jewish Christian phenomenon: all its members were Jews.[349] That the controversy dealt with by the First Church Council at Jerusalem was whether a person could become a follower of Jesus without first effectively converting to Judaism (i.e., without observing the ceremonial law) indicates that the majority opinion in the earliest church was that Jewish Christianity was the norm and that an exception was being made for Gentile Christians. That the apostles were generally supportive of Jewish Christianity should not come as a surprise as they were themselves Jewish Christians. Jewish Christianity was the conservative practice in the earliest church. Paul's idea—that the Gentiles not be required to observe the ceremonial law—was a liberal, if not radical, concept. However, the apostles evidently found Paul's arguments persuasive and agreed that the requirements of the law would not be laid upon Gentile Christians.[347] It is important to note that the Jerusalem Decree represented a compromise which went deeper than merely dividing up the evangelistic work between Paul and the "pillar apostles." The agreement not only committed the Jewish Christian church in Jerusalem to respect Paul's law-free mission to the Gentiles, it also committed Paul and his Gentile churches to respect the right of the Jewish Christian church to observe the ceremonial law.[350]

---

perspective, the movement toward branding Jewish Christians as heretics, then excommunicating Jewish Christianity as a whole from the larger church took place in of the mutual branding of Judaism and Christianity as heretical to each other and a mutual "excommunication" of each by the other (Boyarin, *Borderlines,* 1-33, 202-225); cf. Annette Yoshiko Reed, "Heresy, Minut, and the 'Jewish-Christian' Novel" in *Jewish-Christianity and the History of Judaism* (Heidelberg, Germany: Mohr Siebeck, 2017), 143-173. *Author's note: In Judaism "minut" is functional equivalent of "heresy" in Christianity. Both refer to theological concepts divergent from the norm.*

[349] Paula Fredriksen, *When Christians Were Jews: The First Generation* (New Haven, CT: Yale University Press, 2018), 1-6.

[350] Craig C. Hill, *Hellenists and Hebrews: Reassessing Division within the Earliest Church* (Minneapolis: Fortress Press, 1992): 146–147.

Even Paul's attitude towards Judaism and Jewish Christianity may have been more open than is popularly believed. In none of Paul's letters does he ever describe himself as a convert from Judaism.[351] Rather, it appears that Paul believed faith in Christ to be the true successor of the faith of Abraham.[352] It can be argued from Paul's own statements that he may have been willing to observe the ceremonial law in his dealings with Jews, if by such means he might win them to Christ.[353] Furthermore, it appears that Paul was willing to require that Gentile converts observe Jewish ethics.[354] Paul does not object to Jewish Christians, but to "Judaizers" (those who attempted to persuade Gentile Christians that the observance of the ceremonial law was necessary for salvation). He did not appear to object to Jewish Christians engaging in ritual practice, as long as they did not believe that it was necessary for their own salvation or anyone else's.[355] It is also instructive on this point that in Paul's letter to the Romans he struggles mightily with and yet is unable to resolve the problem of what will become of most of his Jewish brothers and sisters who have not accepted Jesus as the Messiah. While he recognizes that Jesus is the name by which people are saved, he also recognizes that God's promises of

---

[351] Gal 1:15ff; cf. Phil 3:4ff. In Paul's own account of his coming to faith in Christ, he never calls himself a proselyte nor does he use the term conversion to describe his experience. Rather, he speaks of his experience as a calling. Even in his letter to the Philippians, in which he counts all his achievements as a devout Jew as "loss" and irrelevant to his salvation, he does not renounce his Jewishness or speak of himself as an ex-Jew.

[352] Rom 4:1ff; cf. Patrick J. Hartin, "Jewish Christianity: Focus on Antioch in the First Century," *Scriptura* 36 (1991): 50.

[353] 1 Cor 9:19ff; cf. Acts 21:23–26. The Acts passage, in which Paul agrees to observe the purification rituals while in Jerusalem, is historically problematic. However, in 1 Cor 9:19ff Paul proclaims his willingness to be as a Gentile to Gentiles and as a Jew to Jews. While open to various interpretations, this does allow the possibility that Paul was willing to observe the law occasionally, as a means to an end: winning Jews to Christ. (See Introduction, note 15, for a more complete discussion of this issue.)

[354] Carras, "Jewish Ethics," 306–315.

[355] Rom 14:5f; cf. Roger T. Beckwith, "The Origin of the Festivals Easter and Whitsun," *Studia Liturgica* 13(1979): 7–8. Beckwith argues that Paul allowed Jewish Christians to observe Jewish festivals privately.

salvation to the Jewish people cannot be broken. So, he continues to try to persuade them, but leaves their ultimate fate to God.[356]

III. Clashing Cultures:
The Church in Transition

Even as early as the latter half of the first century, forces were coming into play that pushed the church away from its acceptance of Jewish Christianity as a normative expression of Christianity. The influence of culture permeated the issue from beginning to end. It is clear that a large part of the conflict between the greater church and Jewish Christianity was a conflict between two cultures: Hellenist and Hebrew.[357] Clearly, the changing ethnographic balance of the church had a significant impact on this issue. The earliest church was almost exclusively composed of Jewish Christians. Christians of Gentile origin were few. From the account in the Book of the Acts of the First Jerusalem Council, it is clear that Paul's Hellenistic Christian churches were in the minority, struggling to maintain the position that they need not become Jews in order to become Christians. It is clear from the response of the apostles that their disposition of the controversy is a compromise, with the majority (the Jewish Christian church of Jerusalem) granting the minority (Paul's Hellenistic churches) an exception from the norm.[358]

However, by the end of the first century the ethnic composition of the church had undergone a massive reversal, becoming predominantly Gentile. A variety of external conditions worked to the advantage of the Gentile churches and to the disadvantage of the Jewish Christians. The two Jewish wars, the destruction of Jerusalem, and the exodus of much of the Jewish Christian community from Jerusalem along with their Jewish brothers and sisters, as well as their expulsion from Rome, preoccupied Jewish Christianity at a critical time, suppressing their

---

[356] Rom 9–11.

[357] Hill, 103 ff. However, it must also be noted that this distinction is often overemphasized—by the first century many Jews, especially of the Diaspora, had already become significantly "Hellenized," though still law-observant.

[358] Acts 15:4–30.

development even as the Gentile church flourished. Even so, the Jewish Christian church of Jerusalem had maintained relatively undisputed authority among Christians in Palestine until 135 CE.[359]

At that time, most of the Jewish Christian community, along with its leaders and their Jewish brothers and sisters, left Jerusalem under the expulsion order of Hadrian. After 135 CE, the church in Jerusalem quickly became a predominantly Gentile church with a Hellenistic hierarchy and bishop. From that time onward, the leadership of the Jerusalem church was in the hands of Gentile and mostly non-native bishops. The loss of the See of Jerusalem at this critical time no doubt had significant negative influence on the ability of the Jewish Christians to project their authority.[360] A great number of those Jewish Christians who had left Jerusalem under Hadrian's expulsion order evidently returned very quickly.[361] However, they were now out of power and in the minority. Coincident with the shift in demographics, the fortunes of the two ethnic groups within the church had reversed. By the time of Justin in the middle of the second century, it is clear that the Hellenistic position, once a tolerated minority view, would become the dominant one.[362] It would now be the Jewish Christian churches which would have to defend the position that they need not become Gentiles to remain Christians. It seems an unfortunate fact of human nature that the majority generally assumes that its positions and practices are normative and correct and tends to impose them on the minority.

---

[359] Eusebius, *hist. eccl.* 5.12.1–2. Eusebius enumerates the "bishops of the circumcision" as follows: "The first was James, called the brother of the Lord; after him came Simeon; the third was Justus; the fourth Zaccheus; the fifth Tobias; the sixth Benjamin; the seventh John; the eighth Matthias; the ninth Philip; the tenth Seneca; the eleventh Joseph and the fifteenth and last Jude."

[360] Cf. Eusebius, *hist. eccl.* 4.6.4.

[361] Cf. Epiphanius, *pan.* 29.7.7. (*PE*, 173). Although most of the community fled to Pella of the Decapolis during the war of 70 CE, they quickly returned. Evidently, however, the entire community did not return as indicated by the continued presence of Jewish Christians in the area of Pella until at least the end of the fourth century.

[362] *Dial.* 47.4

IV. The First Easter Controversy

One source of conflict between the Gentile and Jewish Christians in Palestine was the date of the celebration of Easter. Prior to 135 CE, the predominantly Jewish Christian church in Palestine, along with most of the churches of Asia Minor, celebrated Easter on the fourteenth day of Nisan (therefore, they were called *Quartodecimans*). Although they celebrated the Christian Pascha on the same day as the Jews celebrated Pesach (Passover), they did not celebrate it in exactly the same way. They read the biblical Passover stories but interpreted them in a Christian light. While the Jews awaited the arrival of the Messiah, the Jewish Christians awaited his return. In place of the traditional Passover meal, they fasted until the early morning, when they would break the fast with a Eucharist. The fast was both a commemoration of the death of Jesus as the true paschal lamb and a vicarious fast on behalf of the Jews who put him to death.[363]

Around 135 CE, the Gentile leadership of the Jerusalem church decided to shift the celebration of Easter to the Sunday after the fourteenth of Nisan. Wilson argues that this was, at least in part, a deliberate move to dissociate Christianity from Judaism, a move colored with anti-Jewish attitudes. Disputes over the date of Easter would continue to erupt over the next several centuries and anti-Jewish attitudes would continue to be one of the many forces at work in these controversies.[364]

V. Jewish Christianity on the Defensive

By the time of Justin Martyr in the mid-second century, it is apparent that another shift has occurred. In his *Dialogue with Trypho the Jew*,

---

[363] Eusebius, *hist. eccl.* 5.24.24 14–16; Epiphanius, *pan.* 70.9–10; *Didascalia* 21; cf. S. G. Wilson, "Passover, Easter, and Anti-Judaism," *To See Ourselves as Others See Us: Christians Jews, and "Others" in Late Antiquity,* ed. Jacob Neusner and Ernest S. Frerichs (Chico, CA: Scholars Press, 1955): 340. (Hereafter, quotes from Wilson's text shall be referred to by the initials *PEAJ.*)

[364] Eusebius, *hist. eccl.* 4–6.4; Epiphanius, *pan.* 70.9–10; cf. Wilson, *PEAJ,* 340f.

written after 155 CE, Justin refers to Jewish Christians, or, as he describes them, "those who wish to observe such institutions as were given by Moses...along with their hope in Christ...yet choose to live with the Christians and the faithful." He makes the case that the ceremonial law has become impracticable, at least in part, due to the destruction of the temple, and that it is of no importance. However, he admits that Jews who follow Christ may choose to observe such rituals without detriment to their own salvation as long as they do not impose them upon Gentile Christians by representing them as necessary for salvation.[365] Justin even goes so far as to say that even if a Gentile convert were, at the instigation of a Jewish Christian, to submit to the ceremonial law, the convert would still be saved.[366] Following the ceremonial law was only dangerous if it led a person to return to normative Judaism and to reject Jesus as the Messiah.[367] Justin believed that following the Jewish rituals was perhaps ineffective, but certainly not sinful or heretical. It was Justin's belief that the church should join itself with Jewish Christians "and associate with them in all things as kinsmen and brethren."[368]

Yet it is clear that by Justin's time things have changed. While Justin's position would have been close to the conservative point of view in the first century, by the middle of the second century it had become a liberal point of view. In fact, Justin acknowledges that there are increasing numbers of Christians who are less tolerant than he is on the issue of Jewish ritual, who refuse to speak to Jewish-Christians, and who deny that they have any hope of salvation.[369] While in the first century it was the Hellenistic Christians who had, with some difficulty, gained acceptance from the Jewish Christian majority of a law-free Christianity for Gentiles, it was now Jewish Christians who were struggling for acceptance, and perhaps even survival. In retrospect, it is clear that in Justin's day the church reached a turning point in its attitude toward Jewish Christianity. Although Jewish Christianity was still within the

---

[365] *Dial.* 47.1–3, quoted in Pritz, *Nazarene*, 19f; cf. Acts 15:1–24. Note the similarities to the Jerusalem formula of the previous century.

[366] *Dial.* 47.4, quoted in Pritz, *Nazarene,* 19f.

[367] *Dial.* 47.4ff, quoted in Pritz, *Nazarene,* 19f.

[368] *Dial.* 47, quoted in Pritz, *Nazarene,* 19f.

[369] *Dial.* 47.4, quoted in Pritz, *Nazarene,* 19f.

greater church, a shift in attitude had begun which would eventually result in the complete excommunication of Jewish Christianity.

VI. The Easter Controversy Continued:
Anti-Judaism and Politics

Issues surrounding the celebration of Easter continued to be a source of controversy beyond Justin's day. Around 167 CE, Bishop Melito of Sardis composed an Easter homily.[370] Melito's *Homily* is illustrative of the attitudes which colored the relationship between the Gentile and Jewish churches. Although Melito may have been a Quartodeciman himself, he appeared to be under heavy pressure to distinguish the Christian and Jewish festivals.[371] In his reply, he does so in several ways. In the first part of the *Homily*, he makes extreme supercessionary claims, appropriating not only the Passover but all of Israel's traditions to the church and denying them to Israel.[372] All of the possessions of Israel—the People, the Law, the Holy City, the Temple, and the Covenant—now belonged to the church.[373] With the appearance of the "reality" (Christ), the "model" (Israel) is "useless... abolished... worthless... made void."[374] Judaism is now defunct.

The second part of Melito's *Homily* dealt with the fall and its effects: sin and death. The third part dealt with Christ's death.[375] However, although some of the text deals with the benefits of Christ's death in overcoming sin and death,[376] most of the text is an

---

[370] Melito, *Homily on the Passion*, quoted in Wilson, *PEAJ*, 343–347. Melito's *Homily* is the earliest known Easter homily.)

[371] Eusebius, *hist. eccl.* 5.24.2–6; cf. Wilson, 350.

[372] *Pascha* 1.224–244; 2.255–279 (*PEAJ*, 344); cf. Wilson, *Anti-Judaism*, 345f.

[373] *Pascha* 2.280–300 (*PEAJ*, 345); cf. Wilson, 345f.

[374] *Pascha* 1.224–244; 2.255–279 (*PEAJ*, 344); cf. Wilson, *Anti-Judaism*, 345f.

[375] Wilson, *Anti-Judaism*, 346.

[376] *Pascha* 2.763–804 (*PEAJ*, 346); cf. Wilson, *Anti-Judaism*, 346ff.

emotional indictment of Israel for the crime of deicide: the killing of their God.[377]

> An unprecedented murder has occurred in the middle of
> Jerusalem, in the city of the law,
> in the city of the Hebrews,
> in the city of the prophets,
> in the city accounted just.[378]

> He who hung the earth is hanging;
> he who fixed the heavens has been fixed;
> he who fastened the universe has been fastened to a tree;
> the Sovereign has been insulted;
> the God has been murdered;
> the King of Israel has been put to death by an Israelite right
> hand.[379]

Melito accused all of Israel, making no distinction between leader and people, between Palestinian and Diaspora Jews, between past and present Jews. He accused them not merely of blindness, but of malevolence: rejecting Jesus precisely because he was just and compassionate[380] and joyfully celebrating the Passover while he died.[381] In rejecting Christ, they rejected God, their election as the people of God, and their salvation. In doing so they earned God's rejection and the punishment of bitterness and death.[382] The guilt of the Jews is intensified further by the absence of any mention of Pilate and the Romans in connection with Christ's death.

By Melito's way of thinking, the very existence of Jews was an implicit challenge to Christianity's appropriation of the traditions of Israel. Affirmation of Christian belief meant the denial of the

---

[377] *Pascha* 2.551–762 (*PEAJ*, 346); cf. Wilson, *Anti-Judaism*, 346ff. Wilson notes that this homily has earned Melito the title "The First Poet of Deicide."

[378] *Pascha* 2.693–697 (*PEAJ*. 347); cf. Wilson, *Anti-Judaism*, 348.

[379] *Pascha* 2.711–716 (*PEAJ*, 347); cf. Wilson, *Anti-Judaism*, 348.

[380] *Pascha* 2.505f, 545f (*PEAJ*, 348); cf. Wilson, *Anti-Judaism*, 348.

[381] *Pascha* 2.566f (*PEAJ*, 348); cf. Wilson, *Anti-Judaism*, 348.

[382] *Pascha* 2.680f; 744f (*PEAJ*, 348); cf. Wilson, *Anti-Judaism*, 348.

equivalent Jewish belief.[383] The fact that he traveled to Palestine for consultation on the Hebrew Bible, rather than consulting members of the sizeable Jewish population on Sardis, underscores his antipathy toward Judaism.[384] If some members of his congregation were abandoning Christianity in favor of Judaism, as some early documents suggest, this would have only intensified the threat he felt from Judaism.[385] This powerful current of anti-Judaism, even as expressed by a Quartodeciman such as Melito, goes a long way toward explaining the growing antipathy of the Gentile church toward Jewish Christians, who claimed to follow Christ but who observed the law. In many ways, the existence of Jewish Christians would have been even more abhorrent to supercessionist thinkers than the existence of synagogue Jews since their very existence as Christians who remain Jews (rather than giving up their Jewishness) would negate his supercessionist theology.

By the end of the second century, there is evidence of open dispute between the Hellenistic church authorities in Jerusalem, under Bishop Narcissus and his successor, Bishop Alexander, and the Jewish Christians.[386] Again, the controversy was over the dating of Easter. Despite the earlier introduction of the practice of celebrating Easter on the Sunday after the fourteenth of Nisan, the Gentile and Jewish churches in Palestine continued to celebrate Easter on two different dates. The churches associated with Rome observed it on a Sunday (calculated independently of the fourteenth of Nisan). The Jewish Christian churches along with most of the other churches of Asia Minor (which were Gentile Christian congregations) still observed it on the fourteenth of Nisan.[387]

---

[383] Wilson, *Anti-Judaism*, 349.

[384] Eusebius, *hist. eccl.* 4.26.14 (*PEAJ*, 351); cf. Wilson, *Anti-Judaism*, 351.

[385] Ignatius, *phil.* 6.1 (*PEAJ*, 351); cf. Wilson, *Anti-Judaism*, 351.

[386] Eusebius, *hist. eccl.* 5.23.5; 5.24.2–6; quoted in Bagatti, *Church from the Circumcision,* 80.

[387] Wilson, *Anti-Judaism*, 339; Bagatti, 80; Beckwith, 1ff. Both sides of the dispute had good reasons for their traditions. The Roman churches preferred Sunday because that was the day on which Christ's Resurrection occurred. The Jewish Christians and other Quartodecimans preferred the fourteenth of Nisan because, according to the Gospel of John, that was the date on which the paschal lamb was sacrificed and when Christ's crucifixion

The diversity of dates for the celebration of Easter created a good deal of confusion among the churches. The confusion was even more pronounced in those areas, such as Palestine, which at the same time contained different churches associated with both traditions. In 196 CE, Bishop Victor of Rome, perceiving such public disagreement as unseemly, moved to enforce uniformity.[388] A move towards uniformity was not in itself undesirable to the parties involved. However, the way in which he moved to achieve that goal suggests ulterior motives. He ordered regional synods to be held, at which a unified date for the celebration of Easter would be promulgated. The Palestinian synod was held at Caesarea. Only Gentile bishops associated with Rome were in attendance. Whether the Jewish Christian bishops were purposely omitted or chose not to attend cannot be determined from available evidence. What is known is that Jewish Christian opinions on the subject were not heard. Not surprisingly, the Palestinian synod decided upon the Western usage. Understandably, the attempts of Bishop Narcissus and his successor Bishop Alexander to implement this change met with considerable resistance from Jewish Christians.[389] Clement of Alexandria records that Alexander had to appeal to him for assistance in defending the change.[390] Eventually, the issue was dropped without resolution. From his heavy-handed attempt to promulgate the Roman usage, it would appear that Victor's motives may have included the assertion of the primacy of Rome.[391] From the exclusion of Jewish Christian representatives from the synod it would appear to represent at least a power struggle between the Gentile and Jewish Christian communities, and perhaps an expression of the anti-Judaistic sentiment which was continuing to grow within the Gentile church.[392]

---

occurred. The actual origins of Easter are shrouded in obscurity. The Jewish Christian practice of Quartodecimanism was probably the more ancient of the two, depending on the apostolic authority of John for its origin.

[388] C. J. Hefele, *A History of the Councils of the Church, Vol. 1, To AD 325* (Edinburgh, T. & T. Clark, 1871): 80ff; cf. Wilson, *Anti-Judaism*, 343.

[389] Bagatti, 80f; Wilson, *Anti-Judaism*, 339f.

[390] See Bagatti, 10.

[391] Wilson, *Anti-Judaism*, 343.

[392] Wilson, *Anti-Judaism*, 343.

VII. Irenaeus and the Ebionites:
The First Excommunications

By the beginning of the third century the excommunication of
Jewish Christianity had begun in fact. Writing around the same time
that the synod of Caesarea was dealing with the dispute over the date
of Easter, Irenaeus began the process of excommunicating the
Jewish Christians by declaring the Ebionites to be heretical,
although not based on the practice of the law. Rather, Irenaeus
judged them based on their theology to have rejected God by their
own beliefs: "not receiving God so as to have union with him."[393]

Irenaeus was no doubt correct in placing the Ebionites
outside the church. Their theology was heretical, they rejected
apostolic authority, and they rejected large portions of the Scripture.
But the excommunication of the Ebionites was problematic for a
different reason. By the middle of the third century, there is evidence
of a growing tendency on the part of the church fathers to confuse
the various Jewish Christian groups and lump them together under
the name Ebionite, regardless of their actual doctrines.[394] This
tendency was no doubt a result of the continually decreasing contact
between the Gentile and Jewish churches, as the geographic center
of authority shifted away from Jerusalem. It seems inevitable that
the increasing distance (both geographic and social) between the
Gentile church fathers and Jewish Christianity would increase the
likelihood that the church fathers might misunderstand Jewish
Christian practices and beliefs. This unfortunate trend would
continue into the next century and beyond.[395] Only three of the
church fathers (Origen, Epiphanius, and Jerome) actually wrote
from Palestine, and even they appeared to have had little social
contact with the Jewish Christian groups of which they wrote.

---

[393] *adv. haer.* 5.1.3 (*PE*, 107); cf. 4.33.4 (*PE*, 107).

[394] Origen, *c. Celsum* 5.61 (*PE*, 135); cf. 5.65; *in Matth.* 16.12 (*PE*, 131).

[395] Eusebius, *onomas.* 172.1–3 (*PE*, 151).

VIII. Nicaea and the Easter Decree:
The Axe is Raised

In the third and fourth centuries there is evidence of continuing disputes over Easter and increasing hostility towards those who, like the Jewish Christians, combined Jewish and Christian practices.[396] Earlier in the life of the church, while the church was still immersed in the battle with paganism and still faced persecution under the Roman Empire, there appeared to be a far greater tolerance for diversity.[397] By the beginning of the fourth century, the church—no longer under persecution and having won its battle with paganism (or at least achieved a beachhead)—was freed to focus on its own organization. There was a strong desire to reorganize the church in the interests of promoting visible unity. The leaders of the greater church, by and large, had come to view Jewish practices and traditions as one of the major causes of division in the church.

The Council of Nicaea, held in 325 CE, is perhaps most widely known for its denunciation of Arianism. Less widely known, but of pivotal significance to the fate of Jewish Christianity, are its actions concerning the date of the celebration of Easter. There was no detailed record made of the actual debates on this subject. However, the decree of the Council on the subject, along with Emperor Constantine's accompanying letter, shed some light on the attitudes behind the decision. Excerpts from both the decree of the Council of Nicaea and Emperor Constantine's letter follow in order.

From the decree:

All the brethren who are in the East who formerly celebrated Easter with the Jews who from ancient times have celebrated the feast at the same time as the Romans, with us and with all those

---

[396] Wilson, *Anti-Judaism*, 341; Bagatti, 86f.

[397] Witness Justin Martyr's tolerant attitudes towards Jewish Christians and the attempts of apologists generally to define and defend Christianity in terms understandable to those of other points of view. On the other hand, it could be argued that this may not reflect tolerance so much as necessity.

who from ancient times have celebrated the feast at the same time as us.[398]

From Constantine's letter:

When the question relative to the sacred festival of Easter arose, it was universally thought that it would be convenient that all should keep it on one day; for what could be more beautiful and desirable than to see this festival, through which we receive the hope of immortality, celebrated by all-in-one accord, and in the same manner? It was declared to be particularly unworthy for this, the holiest of all festivals, to follow the custom (the calculation) of the Jews, who had soiled their hands with the most fearful of crimes, and whose minds were blinded. In rejecting their custom, we may transmit to our descendants the legitimate mode of celebrating Easter, which we have observed from the time of the Savior's Passion to the present day (according to the day of the week). We ought not therefore to have anything in common with the Jews, for the Savior has shown us another way: our worship follows a more legitimate and more convenient course (the order of the days of the week); and consequently, in unanimously adopting this mode, we desire dearest brethren to separate ourselves from the detestable company of the Jews, for it is truly shameful for us to hear them boast that without their direction they could not keep this feast?...How, then, could we follow these Jews, who are most certainly blinded by error?...But even if this were not so, it would still be your duty not to tarnish your soul by communications with such wicked people (the Jews). Besides, consider well, that in such an important matter, and on a subject of such great solemnity, there ought not to be any division. Our Savior has left us only one festal day of our redemption, that is to say, of His holy passion, and He desired (to establish) only one Catholic Church. Think, then, how unseemly it is, that on

---

[398] *Nicaea,* Canon 20; Wilson, 341; cf. Norman P. Tanner, ed., *Decrees of the Ecumenical Councils. Vol. 1, Nicaea I to Lateran V* (Washington, DC: Georgetown University Press, 1990): 19.

the same day some should be fasting, while others are seated at the banquet; and that after Easter, some should be rejoicing at feasts, while others are still observing a strict fast. For this reason, Divine Providence wills that this custom should be rectified and regulated in a uniform way; and everyone, I hope will agree upon this point. As, on the one hand, *it is our duty not to have anything in common with the murderers of our Lord*, and as, on the other, the custom now followed by the Churches of the West, of the South, and of the North, and by some of the East, is the most acceptable, it has appeared good to all…You should consider not only that the number of churches in these provinces make a majority, but also that it is right to demand what reason approves, and that *we should have nothing in common with the Jews.*[399] [Italics by author]

The Quartodeciman practice of celebrating Easter on the fourteenth of Nisan was now banned. Only the Roman practice of the Sunday celebration of Easter was to be allowed. Taken together, the decree and the accompanying letter illustrate the complex motives behind the decision: from well-intentioned theological and pastoral considerations to political considerations to outright anti-Jewish attitudes.[400] On the one hand, they illustrate a desire to overcome confusion and disunity; these are valid concerns, especially when they concern the primary festal day of the church. Secondly, they demonstrate that the supercessionist theology expressed by Melito of Sardis was still current at the time of Nicaea. If such a theology is accepted (if Christ fulfills, supersedes, and nullifies Israel), then it would be unacceptable for the church to be in the position of having the date of its most holy day set by the leaders of the Jews,

---

[399] Eusebius, *Const.* 3.18–20, quoted in Hefele, *Vol. 1,* and 323f.

[400] Cf. *Jud.* 2–3; *chron. Pasch.* 6–7 (*PEAJ,* 342); Aphrahat, *dem.* 3, 12 (*PEAJ,* 342); Wilson, *Anti-Judaism*, 342. Wilson argues that the attitudes expressed in the Nicene decree and the accompanying letter from Constantine were typical of the attitudes surrounding the Easter controversies, running from supercessionist theologies, through denial of the legality of the Jewish Passover, to outright vilification.

putting Christianity in a position of dependence relative to Judaism.[401]

On the other hand, these documents demonstrate that strong anti-Jewish attitudes lay behind the decision. Constantine repeatedly argued that the church should have nothing to do with the Jews, whom he variously accused of being sinful, criminal, blind, detestable, and wicked. Furthermore, he repeats Melito of Sardis's charges of deicide, accusing the Jews of being the "murderers of our Lord."[402] That Constantine also had the political motive to unify the Roman Empire using common religious practices goes without saying.

The argument can be made that this decision expressed an antipathy to Jewish Christianity that was perhaps even stronger than that held against the synagogue Jews. Jacob Neusner argues that by the fourth century the confrontation between Christianity and Judaism had ceased to be a direct discussion. Rather, each used the other for polemical purposes, framing their respective discussions in terms irrelevant to the other party. Neusner argues that the debate at Nicaea was not framed in terms with which synagogue Jews would have been familiar.[403] Rather, it was aimed at those within the church, like the Jewish Christians, who tried to hold onto the traditions of both Judaism and Christianity. Evidence that the decision was aimed against Jewish Christianity can also be seen in the records of who attended the council. Simply stated, the Jewish

---

[401] Wilken, Robert L. "The Restoration of Israel in Biblical Prophecy: Christian and Jewish Responses in the Early Byzantine Period," in *"To See Ourselves as Others See Us": Christians, Jews, "Others" in Late Antiquity*, ed. Jacob Neusner and Ernest S. Frerichs (Chico, CA: Scholars Press, 1985): 466f. Wilken notes that this was a common idea in the theology of the time, expressed by Theodoret, Jerome, and others. In fairness, it should also be noted that anti-Judaism in early Christianity did not spring up in a vacuum. Christian anti-Judaism arose, at least in part, as a defensive response to active criticism of the church among the Jews.

[402] Eusebius, *Const.* 3.18–20, quoted in Hefele, Vol. 1, 324.

[403] Neusner, Jacob. *Judaism and Christianity in the Age of Constantine: History, Messiah, Israel, and the Initial Confrontation* (Chicago: University of Chicago Press: 1987): 143; cf. Gerald Bonner, *Review of "Judaism and Christianity in the Age of Constantine: History, Messiah, Israel, and the Initial Confrontation,"* by Jacob Neusner, in *Theology* 92 (January, 1989): 54–56.

Christians were not invited. Of the 318 fathers at the Council of Nicaea,[404] only eighteen were from Palestine and these were Gentile bishops representing only the coastal cities.[405] No Jewish Christians were in attendance, even though Jewish Christian bishops were still in existence at the time.[406]

The decree of Nicaea notwithstanding, the Quartodeciman practice did not immediately cease even in the Gentile churches. Bagatti argues that the Jewish Christians would have resisted this decision vehemently, not only because of the way it was accomplished, but because they believed that the fourteenth of Nisan date was fixed by the Lord.[407] Therefore, when the church fathers reunited sixteen years later for the Synod of Antioch, they decreed in their first canon that those who continued to follow the Jewish Christian practice would face excommunication:

> All those who do not observe the decision respecting the holy festival of Easter made by the holy and great Synod of Nicaea, assembled in the presence of the most pious Emperor Constantine, are to be excommunicated and cut off from the Church if they continue obstinate in rejecting the legal rule.[408]

With this decree the axe that would eventually cut off Jewish Christianity from the church was poised to fall.

IX. Gentile and Jewish Christians in Jerusalem: The Holy City in Schism

Meanwhile, in Jerusalem, the Gentile and Jewish Christian communities appear to have totally separated from each other, with the Gentile bishops installed at the Holy Sepulcher and the Jewish

---

[404] Tanner, *Decrees of the Ecumenical Councils*, 1. Tanner notes that 318 is the traditional figure given by Hilary of Poitiers. Others recorded figures ranging from 250 to more than 300.

[405] Bagatti, 86f.

[406] Bagatti, 87.

[407] Bagatti, 87.

[408] *Antioch,* Canon I quoted in Hefele, *Vol. 1*; cf. Bagatti, 87.

Christians occupying the Cenacle at Zion,[409] and an "us/them" attitude in evidence between them. Bagatti gives several examples as evidence of the schism, a few of which are offered below. Eusebius spoke of the Christians at Mt. Zion, who "reserve the throne of James" (i.e., the bishopric of James) calling them "those brothers."[410] Jerome discussed the pretended discovery of the body of James on the east side of the Kidron valley and claimed it was "found by one of ours" (a member of the Gentile Christian church, as opposed to a member of the Jewish Christian church).[411] Bagatti suggests that the case for Jewish Christians in residence at Zion is strengthened by the fact that Epiphanius omitted the Cenacle at Zion from his otherwise complete list of the Holy Sites of the Passion, even though the site is associated with the institution of the Eucharist.[412] Similarly, Gregory of Nyssa excluded Zion from his lists of the Holy Sites in Jerusalem. Gregory also noted that certain Jewish Christians in Jerusalem refused to accept him as a true Christian.[413] Clearly, Jerusalem had become a city in schism.

X. Epiphanius and the Nazarenes:
The Axe Falls on Jewish Christianity

By the end of the fourth century, it was no longer acceptable for Jewish Christians to practice any aspects of the ceremonial law, even if they were in all other ways orthodox in belief. By this time, it had become part of the program of the heresiologists to classify Jewish Christian groups as heretical based on orthopraxis, irrespective of orthodoxy (though the two issues are to some degree related). It was at this time that Epiphanius singled out as heretics the Nazarenes, who up to that point apparently had been sufficiently

---

[409] The *Cenacle* at Zion is the traditional site of the Last Supper.

[410] Eusebius, *hist. eccl.* 7.19, quoted in Bagatti, 10.

[411] Jerome, quoted in Bagatti, *Church from the Circumcision,* 10 (complete reference not given).

[412] *anacor.* 40. Also, in the *panarion,* Epiphanius notes that "once the hill of Zion, now lowered, was once more eminent than the Place [Calvary]." Bagatti assumes that this is because it is occupied by Jewish Christians, of whom Epiphanius disapproves.

[413] Gregory of Nyssa, quoted in Bagatti, *Church from the Circumcision,* 11 (complete reference not given).

orthodox in their theology to escape the attention of the heresiologists. From all available evidence, it appears that Epiphanius's decision was based solely on the fact that the Nazarenes practiced the Jewish ceremonial law. By Epiphanius's own account the Nazarenes were in all other ways within the bounds of orthodoxy as he knew it.[414] If the Council of Nicaea had signed the death warrant for Jewish Christianity, then Epiphanius was the executioner. The Nazarenes were perhaps the last "orthodox" Jewish Christian sect in existence. With Epiphanius's declaration of heresy against the Nazarenes (ca. 376 CE), and Augustine's subsequent endorsement (ca. 400 CE), the excommunication of Jewish Christianity from the greater church was complete.[415] Cut off from communion with the church of which they considered themselves a part, even the orthodox Nazarene Jewish Christians eventually faded from existence.

XI. Postscript:
A Broken Promise

The end of this history points back to its beginning. It can be argued that the excommunication of the Nazarenes amounted to a breach of the compromise agreement between Paul and the "pillar apostles" represented by the Jerusalem Decree. In that compromise, the Jewish Christian church in Jerusalem agreed to respect Paul's law-free mission to the Gentiles. Similarly, Paul and the Gentile churches agreed to respect the right of Jewish Christian churches to practice the ceremonial law. The Nazarenes were the descendants of the Jewish Christian church of Jerusalem. They considered themselves a part of the greater Church. They respected apostolic authority. They acknowledged the authority of Paul, his letters, and

---

[414] *pan.* 29 (*PE*, 169–175). Epiphanius could find no heretical doctrines among the beliefs of the Nazarenes. He recognized them as the direct descendants of the original Jerusalem congregation. He acknowledged the fact that they considered themselves a part of the greater church. In addition, they did not view the ceremonial law as essential for salvation and did not require it of Gentile converts.

[415] Epiphanius, *pan.* 29.7.1 (*PE*, 173); Augustine, *de bapt.* 7.1.1 (*PE*, 237).

law-free Gentile mission. Yet they reserved to themselves the right to practice the ceremonial law, not for purposes of salvation, but to be imitators of their Lord and Savior, Jesus Christ.[416] It clearly can be argued that while the Nazarene Jewish Christians yet honored the decree, it was broken by the larger Church.

XII. Summary and Conclusions

The history of the relationship between the Gentile Christian church and Jewish Christians was long and complex. Many factors wove themselves together over several centuries, pushing the two communities apart. Two Jewish wars and the expulsion of Jews and Jewish Christians from Jerusalem began the separation of the communities. The return of the Jewish Christians to find that a Gentile Christian hierarchy had been established in Jerusalem and that "foreign" practices of Easter celebration had been established created tension between the communities. Increasing distance and lack of interaction between the communities resulted in confusion and misunderstanding in the Gentile church regarding the theology and practices of Jewish Christians. Well-intentioned theological and pastoral concerns, combined with growing anti-Jewish attitudes and Rome's interests in asserting its primacy, especially around the issue of the timing of the Easter celebration, increasingly drove the Gentile church toward a final break with Jewish Christianity. In the end, when the Gentile Christian church excommunicated the last remaining orthodox Jewish Christian group, it only reflected the near complete schism which had already come to exist between them.

---

[416] Epiphanius, *pan.* 29.7.2 (*PE*, 173); cf. 1 Cor 11; Eph 5:1; 1 Thess 1:6. As previously described, Epiphanius noted that the Nazarenes accepted the letters of the Apostle Paul, while the Ebionites rejected them. Therefore, it seems unlikely that the Ebionites would have used such a characteristically Pauline phase as "imitators of Christ." The most likely explanation is that Origen has confused the two groups and mistakenly attributed this motivation to the Ebionites.

6

Conclusions

It was this author's thesis that, within the diversity which characterized the Jewish Christianity of the early church, there existed at least one Jewish Christian sect whose theology stood within the acceptable boundaries of orthodoxy of the greater church, and that this sect existed through at least the fourth century, at which point it was declared heretical by the church fathers and eventually died out, despite the fact that it remained within the bounds of orthodoxy[415] and considered itself a part of the greater church. This thesis has been borne out by the results of this study. Though there appears to have been at least one heretical Jewish Christian sect (i.e., the Ebionites),[416] there also appears to have been at least one group whose theology was essentially orthodox. The Nazarenes were that group. Writing in the later part of the fourth century, Epiphanius could find nothing about their theology or Christology that violated the standards of orthodoxy of his time. The Nazarene doctrine of God was fundamentally Trinitarian[417] and they appear to have

---

[415] That is, orthodox in all ways except for its observance of the ceremonial law.

[416] For the reasons listed in the Introduction, it is impossible to determine the precise number of heretical Jewish Christian sects. Although the Ebionite sect was described by the church fathers as a single heretical Jewish Christian sect, it is likely that it represented at least two or three related groups, at least one of which may not have been heretical.

[417] The Nazarene doctrine of the Holy Spirit, though it may have been somewhat primitive and underdeveloped, was not heretical. Even the greater church's doctrine of the Holy Spirit took significantly longer than the other doctrines to develop, not reaching its final form until the fourth or fifth century. That the Nazarene doctrine of the Holy Spirit might have been somewhat primitive compared to that of the greater church would not be unexpected. The increasing isolation of the Nazarenes would have cut them off from the deliberations and decisions of the greater church on this issue, accounting for the slower development of this doctrine among the Nazarenes.

essentially grasped the dual nature of Jesus Christ.[418] Patristic evidence also indicates that the Nazarenes accepted the authority of the Apostle Paul, his Gentile mission, his epistles, and the entirely of the Scriptures as they existed at the time. They also appear to have considered themselves a part of the greater church, acknowledging both apostolic authority[419] and the church's evangelistic mission.[420] Furthermore, although they practiced the ceremonial law, they did not consider it essential for salvation, nor did they require it of Gentile converts. Rather, they practiced the law to be "imitators of Christ."[421] Apparently, it was solely on the basis of their practice (e.g., observance of the ceremonial law) that Epiphanius and those who came after him declared the Nazarenes to be heretical. Although Epiphanius did not clearly state his reasons for declaring the Nazarenes heretical, he probably did so on the basis that their continued practice of Jewish traditions violated the decrees of the Council of Nicaea (325 CE) and the Synod of Antioch (341 CE) and, as such, were grounds for excommunication.[422]

As described by Epiphanius, the Nazarenes appeared to be perhaps the sole representatives of theological orthodoxy among the Jewish Christian groups in Palestine at the time, at least of those groups known to exist. The archaeological evidence, however, as interpreted by Bagatti and Mancini, appears to present a different picture. Based on the prevalence of Jewish Christian symbols at a wide variety of sites (e.g., Jerusalem, Bethlehem, Nazareth and the

---

[418] Fragments from the Nazarene gospel which refer to the baptism of Jesus show Jesus affirming both sinlessness and limited foreknowledge. Epiphanius noted that he was unable to determine whether or not the Nazarenes' gospel included the infancy narratives (unlike the Ebionites, who were known to have excised them to eliminate possible references to the divine nature of Jesus Christ). However, earlier authors, not mentioning the Nazarenes by name but most likely describing them, affirmed that their gospel did include the infancy narratives.

[419] As opposed to the Ebionites, who by various accounts rejected the writings of Paul, various portions of Scripture, and the authority of the apostolic church.

[420] The Jewish Talmudic evidence supports the patristic evidence on this point, preserving the memory of Nazarene Jewish Christians evangelizing their brothers and sisters in the synagogues.

[421] Origen, *in Matth.* Ser 79 (*PE*, 131).

[422] *Antioch,* Canon 1, quoted in Hefele; *Vol. 1*; cf. Bagatti, 87.

hill country of Galilee, the Transjordan, and other areas), Bagatti and Mancini suggest that Jewish Christian groups were far more prevalent than the patristic sources allow. In fact, they suggest that Jewish Christianity may have been dominant in Palestine until the arrival of the Byzantines.

This discrepancy cannot be entirely resolved on the basis of existing evidence. But it is possible to speculate. On the one hand, it is entirely possible that Jewish Christians may have been present in larger numbers than the patristic evidence would seem to indicate. Certainly, the increasing social distance and power struggles between Gentile and Jewish Christian churches in Palestine (as well as between Christianity and Judaism generally) would account for some underrepresentation by the church fathers. Furthermore, once the church fathers had declared Jewish Christianity heretical, it would have suited their purposes to portray Jewish Christian groups in such a way as to minimize their prevalence and to paint them as a fringe group.

On the other hand, there are some difficulties in accepting the data of Bagatti and Mancini. The archeological evidence is such that it cannot be used to shed any light on the composition or the theology of any Jewish Christian group.[423] In some of the sites it is equally possible that the Jewish Christian symbols could have been made either by bona fide Jewish Christians or Gentile Christians with a preoccupation with Jewish observance (e.g., Judaizing Christians).[424] Furthermore, it is impossible to make any judgments from the archaeological data as to the relative orthodoxy of any specific groups. The resolution of this controversy must await future discoveries, if any. However, there is sufficient evidence to presume

---

[423] Most of the evidence is in the form of Christian and Jewish Christian symbols engraved on tombs, ossuariums, and lamella, or graffiti left on the walls or door lintels of buildings. It is not possible to make definitive identifications of specific groups from such data, although some speculations can be made, based upon the proximity of the sites to the reported locations of certain groups.

[424] However, in many cases the nature of the sites makes it highly unlikely that the graffiti were left by Gentile Christians. For example, Christian symbols left on Jewish family tombs or ossuariums would more likely have been the work of Jewish Christians than Judaizing Gentile Christians.

that Jewish Christian groups may indeed have been more prevalent than the patristic sources indicate.

This author further proposed that the increasing antipathy of the church fathers toward Jewish Christianity was the result of a variety of complex and interrelated influences operating over several centuries. This assertion also appears to be supported by the evidence. While any historical description of the development and interrelationship of the forces which shaped the attitudes of the greater church toward Jewish Christianity can only be sketchy and provisional at best, at least some of the influences can be identified. These included: the changing demographics of the church and the accompanying clash of cultures; the increasing isolation of Jewish Christianity from the predominantly Gentile church; power struggles between competing Christian communities in Palestine as well as Rome's interest in asserting its primacy there; theological and pastoral concerns, which were well-intentioned but which resulted in increasingly narrow views of orthodoxy and orthopraxis; and some outright anti-Jewish feelings.

The case of the Nazarenes seems extremely unfortunate and provides a cautionary note for the church. Orthodox in their theology, considering themselves a part of the apostolic church, yet wanting to retain their Jewish identity, they were marginalized and eventually excommunicated by the greater church because of their ritual practices. The greater church had become so isolated from Jewish Christianity that it focused on their ceremonial practices, while either misinterpreting or ignoring the motives behind those practices. It is a dramatic turnabout. Gentile Christianity itself had once been a misunderstood minority, appealing to the predominately Jewish Christian church authorities at that time for acceptance of its position that it should be free from the requirements of the ceremonial law. Now the tables were turned. Now it was the Gentile Christians who were dominant and the Jewish Christians were on the fringe and in need of understanding. Only this time there was to be no spirit of compromise. It seems an especially poignant tragedy that law-free Gentile Christianity should itself eventually exclude from the church the descendants of the very same Jewish Christian authorities that granted them that freedom. The disappearance of "orthodox" Jewish Christianity from the church (at least in any organized and recognized manner)[425] was not only a tragedy for them but for the church as a whole, because with their disappearance the church lost a vital connection with and source of understanding of its ancient Jewish roots.

The excommunication of Jewish Christianity by the fourth century church raises important questions for the church today. What is our understanding of the Christian faith? Is it fundamentally a relationship with Christ or a set of beliefs and practices? What is our understanding of orthodoxy and orthopraxis, and in what ways do we define ourselves as a Christian community? Do we define ourselves inclusively or exclusively? How do we respond to diversity in the Church? Will we view it as a threat or a blessing? How will we resolve our differences, by dialogue or by excommunication? These are questions that the fourth century church had to ask and answer. How they did so affected the nature of the church for centuries to come. Our own answers to these questions are of no less significance today.

---

[425] But as Jewish scholar Daniel Boyarin notes, "there are Christian who are Jews, or perhaps better put. Jews who are Christians, even up to this day." (Boyarin, Borderline, 225).

Bibliography

Bagatti, Bellarmino. *The Church from the Circumcision: History and Archaeology of the Judaeo-Christians*. Jerusalem: Franciscan, 1971.

Baur, Ferdinand. *Paul the Apostle of Jesus Christ: His Life and Works; His Epistles and Teachings*, 1845.

Beckwith, Roger T. "The Origin of the Festivals Easter and Whitsun," *Studia Liturgica* 13 (1979): 1–20.

Bonner, Gerald. "Review of Judaism and Christianity in the Age of Constantine: History, Messiah, Israel, and the Initial Confrontation," by Jacob Neusner. In *Theology* 92 (January 1989): 54–56.

Boyarin, Daniel. *Borderlines: The Partition of Judeao-Christianity*. Philadelphia, PA: University of Pennsylvania Press, 2006.

————. *A Radical Jew: Paul and the Politics of Identity*. Berkley, CA: University of California Press, 1994.

Brandon, S. G. F., *The Fall of Jerusalem and the Christian Church: A Study of the Effects of the Jewish Overthrow of AD 70 on Christianity*. London: S.P.C.K., 1957.

Buchanan, George W., "Worship, Feasts and Ceremonies in the Early Jewish Christian Church." *New Testament Studies* 26 (1980): 279-297.

Carras, George P. "Jewish Ethics and Gentile Converts: Remarks on I Thes. 4:3–8." In *The Thessalonian Correspondence*, ed. Raymond F. Collins. Leuven, Belgium: Leuven University, 1990: 306–315

Danielou, Jean. *The Development of Christian Doctrine before the Council of Nicaea. Vol. I, The Theology of Jewish-Christianity*. Chicago: Regnery, 1964.

———. "Review of Archaeological Discoveries Relative to the Jewish-Christians by Ignacio Mancini." In *Recherches de Science Religieuse* 58 (1970): 143–145.

Finkelstein, Louis. "The Development of the Amidah." *Jewish Quarterly Review* 16 (1925–1926): 127–170.

Fitzmyer, Joseph A. "The Qumran Scrolls, the Ebionites and Their Literature." *Theological Studies* 16, no. 3 (1955): 334–372.

———. "Jewish-Christianity in Acts in the Light of the Qumran Scrolls." In *Essays on the Semitic Background of the New Testament*. London: Geoffrey Chapman, 1971.

Fredriksen, Paula. *When Christians Were Jews: The First Generation*. New Haven, CT: Yale University Press, 2018.

Fuller, Reginald H. "Matthew" in *Harper's Bible Commentary*, ed. James L. Mays, 951–982. San Francisco: Harper and Row, 1988.

Getty, Mary Ann. "Paul and the Salvation of Israel." *Catholic Bible Quarterly* 50 (1988): 456-469.

Hahn, Robert R. "The Undivided Way: Early Jewish Christians as a Model for Ecumenical Encounter?" *Journal of Ecumenical Studies* 14, no. 4 (1977): 233-248.

————. "Judaism and Christianity at Antioch: Charisma and Conflict in the First Century." *Journal of Religious History* 14, no. 4 (1987): 341-360.

Hartin, Patrick J. "Jewish Christianity: Focus on Antioch in the First Century." *Scriptura* 36 (1991): 38–50.

Hefele, C. J. *A History the Councils of the Church. Vol. 1, To AD 325.* Edinburgh: T. & T. Clark, 1871.

————. *A History the Councils of the Church. Vol. 2, AD 325 to AD 429.* Edinburgh: T. & T. Clark, 1871.

Hill, Craig C. *Hellenists and Hebrews: Reassessing Division within the Earliest Church.* Minneapolis: Fortress, 1992.

Josephus, Flavius. *The Works of Josephus.* Trans. by William Wiston. Peabody, MA: Hendrickson, 1987.

Katz, Steven T. "Issues in the Separation of Judaism and Christianity after 70 CE: A Reconsideration." *Journal of Biblical Literature* 103, no. 3 (1984): 43-76.

Klein, Charlotte. *Anti-Judaism in Christian Theology.* Trans. by Edward Quinn. Philadelphia, PA: Fortress Press.

Klijn, Albertus F. J. "The Study of Jewish-Christianity." *New Testament* 20 (1973/74): 419–431.

————. "Jewish Christianity in Egypt." In *The Roots of Egyptian Christianity*, ed. A. B. Pearson and J. E. Goehring, 167-177. Philadelphia, PA: Fortress Press.

————. *Jewish Christian Gospel Tradition.* Leiden, Netherlands: E. J. Brill, 1973

Klijn, Albertus F. J., and Gerrit J. Reinink. *Patristic Evidence for Jewish Christian Sects*. Leiden, Netherlands: E. I. Brill, 1973.

Koester, Craig R. "The Origin and Significance of the Flight to Pella Tradition." *The Catholic Bible Quarterly* 51 (1989): 90–106.

Lightfoot, J. B. *The Apostolic Fathers* (New York: Olms, 1973)

Longenecker, Richard N. *The Christology of Early Jewish Christianity*. London: SCM, 1970.

Lüdemann, Gerd. *Opposition to Paul in Jewish Christianity*. Philadelphia: Fortress, 1989.

Luttikhuizen, G. P. *The Revelation of Elchasai: Investigations into the Evidence for a Mesopotamian Jewish Apocalypse of the Second Century and Its Reception by Judeo-Christian Propagandists*. Tubingen, Germany: J. C. B. Mohr, 1985.

Mancini, Ignazio. *Archaeological Discoveries Relative to the Judaeo-Christians*. Jerusalem: Franciscan, 1970.

Mann, J. "Geniza Fragments of the Palestinian Order of Service." *Hebrew Union College Annual* 2 (1925), 269–338.

Marcus, Joel, "The Circumcision and the Uncircumcision in Rome." *New Testament Studies* 35 (1989): 67-81.

Martin, J. Louis. "Paul and His Jewish-Christian Interpreters." *Union Seminary Quarterly Review* 15 (1987): 1-15.

Meyers, E. M. "Early Judaism and Christianity in the Light of Archaeology." *Biblical Archaeology* 51, no. 2 (1988), 69–79.

Neusner, Jacob. *Judaism and Christianity in the Age of Constantine: History, Messiah, Israel, and the Initial Confrontation.* Chicago: University of Chicago, 1987.

Neusner, Jacob. *Why No Gospels in Talmudic Judaism?* Atlanta, GA: Scholars Press, 1988.

Pritz, Raymond A. "The Jewish Christian Sect of the Nazarenes and the Mishnah." In *Proceedings of the Eighth World Congress of Jewish Studies. Division A–The Period of the Bible.* Jerusalem: Magnes, 1981.

———. "On Brandon's Rejection of the Pella Tradition." *Immanuel* 13 (1981), 39–43.

———. *Nazarene Jewish Christianity: From the End of the New Testament Period until Its Disappearance in the Fourth Century.* Jerusalem: Magnes, 1988.

Prybytski, B. "The Setting of Matthean Anti-Judaism." In *Anti-Judaism in Early Christianity. Vol. 1. Paul and the Gospels*, ed. P. Richardson, 181-200. Waterloo, Ontario, Canada: Wilfred Laurier University Press, 1886.

Quispel, Gilles. "The Discussion of Judaic Christianity." *Vigiliae Christianae* 22 (1968): 81–93.

———. "Judaism, Judaic Christianity and Gnosis." In *The New Testament and Gnosis*, ed. A. H. B. Logan and A. J. M. Wedderburn, 45-60. Edinburgh, Scotland: T. and T. Clark, 1983.

Rainbow, Paul. "Jewish Monotheism as the Matrix for New Testament Theology: A Review Article." *Novum Testamentum* 33 (1991): 78-91.

Reicke, B. "Judeo-Christianity and the Jewish Establishment." In *Jesus and the Politics of His Day*, ed. E. Bammel and C. F. D. Moule, 145-152. Cambridge, UK: Cambridge University Press, 1884.

Reed, Annette Yoshiko. *Jewish-Christianity and the History of Judaism*. Heidelberg, Germany: Mohr Siebeck, 2017.

Riegel, Stanley K. "Jewish Christianity: Definitions and Terminology." *New Testament Studies* 24 (1978): 410-415.

Ritschl, Albrecht. *The Formation of the Old Catholic Church* (Second Edition, 1857) Boston, MA: Adamant Media, 2005.

Russell, Walt. "Who Were Paul's Opponents in Galatia?" *Bibliotheca Sacra* 149 (July-September 1980): 329-351.

Saunders, Ernest W. "Jewish Christianity and Palestinian Archeology." *Religious Studies Review* 9, no. 3 (1983): 201–205.

Schechter, Solomon. "Geniza Specimens." *Jewish Quarterly Review* 10 (1897/8): 654–659.

Schiffman, Lawrence H. *Who Was a Jew? Rabbinic and Halakhic Perspectives on the Jewish Christian Schism.* Hoboken: Ktav, 1985.

Schneemelcher, William. "The Gospel of the Egyptians." In *New Testament Apocrypha. Vol. 1, Gospels and Related Writings*, ed. W. Schneemelcher, 209–215. Philadelphia: Fortress, 1991.

Schoeps, Hans-Joachim. *Jewish-Christianity: Factional Disputes in the Early Church.* Philadelphia, PA: Fortress, 1964.

Siker, J. S. *Disinheriting the Jews: Abraham in Early Christian Controversy.* Louisville, KY: Westminster/John Knox Press: 1991.

Simon, Marcel. *Versus Israel: A Study of the Relations between Christians and Jews in the Roman Empire.* Trans. by H. McKeating. New York: Oxford University, 1986.

Stegner, W. R. "Narrative Christology in Early Jewish Christianity." *SBL 1988 Seminar Papers* (1988): 249-262.

————. "Early Jewish Christianity – A Lost Chapter." *Asbury Theological Journal* 44(2) (1989): 17-29.

————. Narrative Christology in Early Jewish Christianity. Louisville, KY: Westminster/John Knox Press: 1989.

————. "The Temptation Narrative: A Study in the Use of Scripture by Early Jewish Christianity." *Biblical Research* 35 (1990): 5-17.

Stendall, Krister. *Paul Among the Jews and Gentiles.* Philadelphia, PA: Fortress Press, 1976.

Strand, Kenneth A. "Sunday Easter and Quartodecimanism in the Early Christian Church." *Andrews University Seminary Studies* 28, no. 2 (Summer 1989): 127-136.

Strecker, Georg. "On the Problem of Jewish Christianity." In *Orthodoxy and Heresy in Earliest Christianity*, ed. W., Bauer, 241-285. Philadelphia, PA: Fortress Press, 1973.

Tanner, Norman P., ed. *Decrees of the Ecumenical Councils. Vol. 1. Nicaea I to Lateran V.* Washington, DC: Georgetown University, 1990.

Velasco, Jesus Maria and Sabourin, Leopold. "Jewish Christianity in the First Centuries." *Biblical Theology Bulletin* 6, no. 1 (February 1976): 5-26.

Vielhauer, Philipp and Georg Strecker. "Jewish-Christian Gospels." In *New Testament Apocrypha. Vol. I, Gospels and Related Writings*, ed. W. Schneemelcher, 134–178. Philadelphia: Fortress, 1991.

von Harnack, Adolf. *History of Dogma. Vol. 1.* Translated by Neil Buchanan. New York: Russell and Russell, 1958.

Wilken, Robert L. John *Chrysostom and the Jews: Rhetoric and Reality in the Late 4th Century.* Berkley, CA: University of California Press, 1983.

———. "The Restoration of Israel in Biblical Prophecy: Christian and Jewish Responses in the Early Byzantine Period." In *"To See Ourselves as Others See Us": Christians Jews, "Others" in Late Antiquity*, ed. Jacob Neusner and Ernest S. Frerichs, 443–471. Chico, CA: Scholars, 1985.

Wilson, Stephen G. "Passover, Easter, and Anti-Judaism: Melito of Sardis and Others." In *"To See Ourselves as Others See Us": Christians, Jews, and "Others" in Late Antiquity*, ed. Jacob Neusner and Ernest S. Frerichs. Chico, CA: Scholars, 1955: 337–356.

———, ed. *Anti-Judaism in Early Christianity. Vol. 2. Separation and Polemic.* Waterloo, Ontario, Canada: Wilfrid Laurier University Press, 1986.

About the Author

The great-grandson of an Orthodox rabbi from Belarus, who thought he might become a rabbi himself, Ken Howard made the "mistake" of betting a college roommate that he could prove Jesus was not the Messiah. He eventually joined the Episcopal Church because it was "the most Jewish church I could find."

Ordained for nearly thirty years in the Episcopal Church, Ken has started two congregations, including the first successful startup congregation in his judicatory in over forty years. He has been involved in several congregational redevelopment projects ever since.

Ken is the founder and Executive Director of The FaithX Project, a faith-based consulting, research, and resource development practice with the mission of helping congregations survive and thrive in challenging times by better understanding and engaging missional opportunities in their communities through data-grounded missional discernment and experimentation.

Ken is also the author of *Paradoxy: Creating Christian Community Beyond Us and Them*, and is currently working on a new book, *The Choice: Faithful Congregational Leadership in Challenging Times*. He is also the author of several published papers, including "The Religion Singularity: A Demographic Crisis Disrupting and Transforming Institutional Christianity" and "Grounding Discernment in Data: Strategic Missional Planning Using GIS Technology and Market Segmentation Data."

Ken and his wife, Rhee, have two adult children, two cats, and a Scottie dog named "Duncan." He and Rhee will soon celebrate forty-six years of marriage. Ken enjoys bike riding, trying new and different ethnic foods, reading science fiction and fantasy, and contemplating the spiritual implications of quantum physics, entangled states, and "spooky action at distance."